THE ANATHEMATA

by the same author

*

IN PARENTHESIS

THE ANATHEMATA

fragments of

an attempted writing

by

DAVID JONES

This prophecie Merlin ſhall make
for I liue before his time

FABER AND FABER LIMITED
3 Queen Square
London

First published in 1952
by Faber and Faber Limited
3 Queen Square, London WC1
Second edition 1955
First published in this edition 1972
Printed in Great Britain by
Latimer Trend & Co Ltd Whitstable
All rights reserved

ISBN 0 571 10127 5

CONTENTS

ILLUSTRATIONS

The lettering on the cover, the two illustrations and the seven inscriptions are reproduced here from much larger originals made by the author. The dates and the media vary, as follows:

PREFACE TO
THE ANATHEMATA

'I have made a heap of all that I could find.'[1] So wrote
Nennius, or whoever composed the introductory matter to
the *Historia Brittonum*. He speaks of an 'inward wound' which
was caused by the fear that certain things dear to him 'should
be like smoke dissipated'. Further he says, 'not trusting my
own learning, which is none at all, but partly from writings
and monuments of the ancient inhabitants of Britain, partly
from the annals of the Romans and the chronicles of the
sacred fathers, Isidore, Hieronymus, Prosper, Eusebius and
from the histories of the Scots and Saxons although our
enemies . . . I have lispingly put together this . . . about past
transactions, that [this material] might not be trodden under
foot.'[2]

Well, although this writing is neither a history of the
Britons nor a history of any sort, and although my intentions
in writing at all could not, I suppose, be more other than
were the intentions of Nennius, nevertheless, there is in
these two apologies which preface his work something which,
in however oblique a fashion, might serve for my apology
also.

Part of my task has been to allow myself to be directed
by motifs gathered together from such sources as have by
accident been available to me and to make a work out of
those mixed data.

---

[1] The actual words are *coacervavi omne quod inveni*, and occur in *Prologue II* to
the *Historia*.

[2] Quoted from the translation of *Prologue I*. See *The Works of Gildas and
Nennius*, J. A. Giles, London, 1841.

This, you will say, is, in a sense, the task of any artist in any material, seeing that whatever he makes must necessarily show forth what is his by this or that inheritance.

True, but since, as Joyce is reported to have said, 'practical life or "art" . . . comprehends all our activities from boat-building to poetry',[1] the degrees and kinds and complexities of this showing forth of our inheritance must vary to an almost limitless extent:

If one is making a table it is possible that one's relationship to the Battle of Hastings or to the Nicene Creed might have little bearing on the form of the table to be made; but if one is making a sonnet such kinds of relationships become factors of more evident importance.

If one is making a painting of daffodils what is *not* instantly involved? Will it make any difference whether or no we have heard of Persephone or Flora or Blodeuedd?[2]

I am of the opinion that it will make a difference, but would immediately make this reservation: Just as Christians assert that baptism by water 'makes a difference', but that many by desire and without water achieve the benefits of that 'difference', so, without having heard of Flora Dea, there are many who would paint daffodils as though they had invoked her by name.

To continue with these three images, 'which I like', that is, the Battle of Hastings, the Nicene Creed and Flora Dea, and to use them—as counters or symbols merely—of the *kind* of motifs employed in this writing of mine; it is clear that if such-like motifs are one's material, then one is trying to make a shape out of the very things of which one is oneself made; even though, as may well be the case, one may be

---

[1] See Gogarty, *As I was Going Down Sackville Street*, p. 287. London, 1937.

[2] Blodeuedd, blod-ei-eth, ei as in height, eth as in nether, accent on middle syllable; from *blodau* flowers. The name given in Welsh mythology to the woman made by magical processes from various blossoms.

aware of these things that have made one, by 'desire' only, and not by 'water'—to pursue the analogy used above.

So that to the question: What is this writing about? I answer that it is about one's own 'thing', which *res* is unavoidably part and parcel of the Western Christian *res*, as inherited by a person whose perceptions are totally conditioned and limited by and dependent upon his being indigenous to this island. In this it is necessarily insular; within which insularity there are the further conditionings contingent upon his being a Londoner, of Welsh and English parentage, of Protestant upbringing, of Catholic subscription.

While such biographical accidents are not in themselves any concern of, or interest to, the reader, they are noted here because they are responsible for most of the content and have had an overruling effect upon the form of this writing. Though linguistically 'English monoglot' accurately describes the writer, owing to the accidents above mentioned certain words, terms and occasionally phrases from the Welsh and Latin languages and a great many concepts and motifs of Welsh and Romanic provenance have become part of the writer's *Realien*, within a kind of Cockney setting. Like the elder boy in *The Prioresses Tale*, who knew well the necessity and significance of the hymn, *Alma Redemptoris Mater*, I too might say:

'I can no more expounde in this matere
I lerne song, I can but smal grammere.'

Seeing that, *as one is so one does*, and that, *making follows being*, it follows that these mixed terms and themes have become part of the making of this writing. But here problems arise and rather grave ones.

The words 'May they rest in peace' and the words 'Whosoever will' might, by some feat of artistry, be so juxtaposed within a context as not only to translate the words 'Requiescant in pace' and 'Quincunque vult' but to evoke the *exact historic over-tones and under-tones* of those Latin words. But should some writer find himself unable by whatever ingenuity of formal arrangement or of contextual allusion to achieve this identity of content and identity of evocation, while changing the language, then he would have no alternative but to use the original form. Such a writer's own deficiency in, or ignorance of, the original language, has only a very limited bearing on the matter, seeing that his duty is to consider only the objective appropriateness of this or that term and its emotive impact within a given context. It is of no consequence to the shape of the work how the workman came by the bits of material he used in making that shape. When the workman is dead the only thing that will matter is the work, objectively considered. Moreover, the workman must be dead to himself while engaged upon the work, otherwise we have that sort of 'self-expression' which is as undesirable in the painter or the writer as in the carpenter, the cantor, the half-back, or the cook. Although all this is fairly clear in principle, I have not found it easy to apply in practice. That is to say I have found it exceptionally hard to decide whether in a given context an 'Whosoever will' is the, so to say, effective sign of a 'Quicunque vult'. Or to give a concrete instance: whether, within its context, my use of the Welsh title 'Gwledig' was avoidable and whether the English translation, 'land-ruler',[1] could have been so conditioned and juxtaposed as to incant what 'Gwledig' incants. The 'grave problems' referred to a few paragraphs back have

---

[1] Or whatever the translation might be. Anwyl's dictionary gives: lord, king, ruler, sovereign, prince. But none of these are satisfactory. The word is connected with *gwlad*, country or land and in modern Welsh *gwledig*, used as an adjective, implies something rural or rustic. As a noun it belongs only to the early Dark Ages; when it was used only of very important territorial rulers; it was used of Maximus the emperor, it was used by Taliessin, of God. Significantly it was never used of Arthur, because he was a leader of a mobile cavalry force, and not a territorial ruler.

mostly arisen over questions of this sort. It must be understood that it is not a question of 'translation' or even of
'finding an equivalent word', it is something much more
complex. 'Tsar' will mean one thing and 'Caesar' another
to the end of time.

When in the Good Friday Office, the Latin, without any
warning, is suddenly pierced by the Greek cry *Agios o Theos*,
the Greek-speaking Roman Church of the third century
becomes almost visibly present to us. So to juxtapose and
condition the English words 'O Holy God' as to make them
do what this change from Latin to Greek effects within this
particular liturgical setting, would not be at all easy. It is
problems of this nature that have occupied me a good deal.

With regard to the actual words in the Welsh language
I have given the meanings and attempted to give the *approximate* sounds in the notes. Welshmen may smile or be angered
at the crudity and amateurishness of these attempts, but
something of the sort was necessary, because in some
cases a constituent part of the actual form—the assonance—
of the writing is affected. I shall give one example of this:
I have had occasion to use the word *mamau*. This key-word
means 'mothers' and can also mean 'fairies'. Now the Welsh
diphthong *au* is pronounced very like the 'ei' diphthong in
the English word 'height'.[1] Hence *mamau* can be made to
have assonance with the Latin word *nymphae* and the English
words 'grey-eyed' and 'dryad', and I have employed these
particular correspondences or near correspondences, on
page 238; but to the reader unacquainted with the Welsh
'au' sound, the form of this passage would be lost. Over such
matters annotation seemed a necessity.

---

[1] For which reason Mr Aneurin Bevan is known as 'Nye' and not 'New'.
The Welsh diphthongs *au* and *eu* have indeed a subtle distinction but not suffi-
cient to affect this matter. The reason being that the Welsh *u* alone has approximately the sound of the English ee in 'bee', hence *au* equals ah + ee.

With regard to the Latin terms employed I have noted the liturgical or other contexts. For many readers these notes may appear to be an elucidation of the obvious, but, on the other hand, we are not all equally familiar with the deposits. It is sometimes objected that annotation is pedantic; all things considered in the present instance, the reverse would, I think, be the more true. There have been culture-phases when the maker and the society in which he lived shared an enclosed and common background, where the terms of reference were common to all. It would be an affectation to pretend that such was our situation today. Certainly it would be an absurd affectation in me to suppose that many of the themes I have employed are familiar to all readers, even though they are, without exception, themes derived from our own deposits. When I read in the deposits we have received from ancient Hebrew sources, of Og, king of Bashan, of the Azazel, of Urim and Thummim, I may or may not wish for further information regarding the significance of this ruler, this daemon and this method of divination. Similarly when in my text I have found it necessary to use the words Laverna and Rhiannon, *Dux Britanniarum* and *Ymherawdr*, *groma* and *hudlath*, it is conceivable that some reader may wish for further information about these two goddesses, two titles and two instruments. I have, therefore, glossed the text in order to open up 'unshared backgrounds' (to use an expression coined by Mr C. S. Lewis),[1] if such they are.

The title-page describes this book as 'fragments of an attempted writing' because that is an exact description of it. It had its beginnings in experiments made from time to time between 1938 and 1945. In a sense what was then written is another book. It has been rewritten, large portions

[1] See commentary by C. S. Lewis, 'Williams and the Arthuriad', in *Arthurian Torso*, 1948.

excluded,[1] others added, the whole rearranged and consider-
ably changed more than once. I find, for instance, that what
is now sheet 166 of my written MS has at different times
been sheet 75 and sheet 7. What is now printed represents
parts, dislocated attempts, reshuffled and again rewritten
intermittently between 1946 and 1951.

The times are late and get later, not by decades but by
years and months. This tempo of change, which in the
world of affairs and in the physical sciences makes schemes
and data out-moded and irrelevant overnight, presents peculiar and phenomenal difficulties to the making of works, and
almost insuperable difficulties to the making of certain kinds
of works; as when, for one reason or another, the making of
those works has been spread over a number of years. The
reason is not far to seek. The artist deals wholly in signs. His
signs must be valid, that is valid for him and, normally, for
the culture that has made him. But there is a time factor
affecting these signs. If a requisite now-ness is not present,
the sign, valid in itself, is apt to suffer a kind of invalidation.
This presents most complicated problems to the artist
working outside a reasonably static culture-phase. These and
kindred problems have presented themselves to me with a
particular clarity and an increasing acuteness. It may be that
the kind of thing I have been trying to make is no longer
makeable in the kind of way in which I have tried to make it.

In the late nineteen-twenties and early 'thirties among my
most immediate friends there used to be discussed something
that we christened 'The Break'. We did not discover the
phenomenon so described; it had been evident in various
ways to various people for perhaps a century; it is now, I
suppose, apparent to most. Or at least most now see that in
the nineteenth century, Western Man moved across a rubicon

[1] Should it prove possible I hope to make, from this excluded material, a
continuation, or Part II of *The Anathemata*.

[15]

which, if as unseen as the 38th Parallel, seems to have been as definitive as the Styx. That much is I think generally appreciated. But it was not the memory-effacing Lethe that was crossed; and consequently, although man has found much to his liking, advantage, and considerable wonderment, he has still retained ineradicable longings for, as it were, the farther shore. The men of the nineteenth century exemplify this at every turn; all the movements betray this if in all kinds of mutually contradictory ways. We are their inheritors, and in however metamorphosed a manner we share their basic dilemmas. 'And how!' as we citizens of the Old Rome say in our new Byzantine lingo from across the Herring Pond.

When in the 'twenties we spoke of this Break it was always with reference to some manifestation of this dilemma *vis-à-vis* the arts—and of religion also, but only in so far as religion has to do with signs, just as have the arts.

That is to say our Break had reference to something which was affecting the entire world of sacrament and sign. We were not however speculating on, or in any way questioning dogma concerning 'The Sacraments'. On the contrary, such dogma was taken by us for granted—was indeed our point of departure. It was with the corollaries, the implications and the analogies of such dogma that we were concerned. Our speculations under this head were upon how increasingly isolated such dogma had become, owing to the turn civilization had taken, affecting signs in general and the whole notion and concept of sign.

Water is called the 'matter' of the Sacrament of Baptism. Is 'two of hydrogen and one of oxygen' that 'matter'? I suppose so. But what concerns us here is whether the poet can and does so juxtapose and condition within a context the formula H_2O as to evoke 'founts', 'that innocent creature', 'the womb of this devine font', 'the candidates', or for that

[16]

matter 'the narrows' and 'the siluer sea, Which serues it in the office of a wall, Or as a Moat defensiue to a house'.

A knowledge of the chemical components of this material water should, normally, or if you prefer it, ideally, provide us with further, deeper, and more exciting significances *vis-à-vis* the sacrament of water, and also, for us islanders, whose history is so much of water, with other significances relative to that. In Britain, 'water' is unavoidably very much part of the *materia poetica*. It may be felt that these examples are somewhat far-fetched, but I choose them as illustrations only. And if you consider how the men of some epochs have managed to wed widely separated ideas, and to make odd scraps of newly discovered data subserve immemorial themes (cf. the English Metaphysicals?)[1] my examples may not appear all that strained.

Whether there is a radical incompatibility between the world of the 'myths' and the world of the 'formulae', or whether it is a matter only of historic accident, of an unfortunate and fortuitous association of ideas leading to estrangement and misunderstanding, are questions which are continually debated and discussed at every sort of level by 'thinkers' of all shades of opinion. Clearly such questions are most grave but they do not directly concern us here, nor are they, I think, within our competence. What we are here concerned with and which does fall within our experience and competence, is the effect and consequence of such unresolved elements (whatever the cause) upon the making of works at this present time; the effect, that is to

---

[1] Who wrote a poetry that was counter-Renaissant, creaturely yet other-world-ordered, ecstatical yet technically severe and ingenious, concerned with conditions of the psyche, but its images very much of the soma; metaphysical, but not un-intrigued by the physics of the period; English, but well represented by names hardly English; thus still posing interesting questions for those specialists whose business it is to research into that epoch. A research which continues. We wish them good hunting.

say, upon ourselves, here and now. We are concerned only with the actual existence of a lesion of some sort (whether ephemeral or more enduring we do not know), which appears, in part at least, to be in some way bound up with the historic phenomena indicated. And we are concerned with the present effects of these phenomena only in so far as those effects impinge upon, raise problems relative to, inconvenience or impoverish, handicap the free use of, modify the possibilities of, or in any way affect the *materia poetica*.

The reader may object, with regard to some of the problems cited, suggested or implied throughout this preface, that they exist only for those who adhere to, or hanker after, some theological scheme; or are otherwise entangled in conceptions and images carried over from a past pattern of life and culture. Though it is easy enough to see how such an objection might seem both cogent and convenient, it arises from a serious misinterpretation of the nature of the problems in question. In case my terminology may be thought by some to lend itself to some such misinterpretation I shall attempt a further elucidation, because it is, in my view, very necessary to get this matter clear.

It might not be a bad idea to remind ourselves here that the attitude of the artist is necessarily empirical rather than speculative. 'Art is a virtue of the practical intelligence.' All 'artistic' problems are, as such, practical problems. You can but cut the suit according to the cloth. For the artist the question is 'Does it?' rather than 'Ought it?'

The problems of which I speak can neither be brought into existence nor made to vanish by your opinions or mine. Though, of course, what we believe, or think we believe, the temper and nature, the validity or otherwise of those beliefs will largely condition our attitude toward all problems. Our beliefs, seeing that they stand in some relationship to the sum of our perceptions, may enhance or lessen our awareness of the very existence of some of those problems. But the problems themselves are inherent in a cultural or civilizational situation, and from problems of such a nature no person of that culture or civilization can escape, least of all the 'poets' of that culture or civilization.

I name the poets in particular, not to round off a phrase, but to state what appears to me to be a fact. The forms and materials which the poet uses, his images and the meanings he would give to those images, his perceptions, what is evoked, invoked or incanted, is in some way or other, to some degree or other, essentially bound up with the particular historic complex to which he, together with each other member of that complex, belongs. But, for the poet, the woof and warp, the texture, feel, ethos, the whole *matière* comprising that complex comprises also, or in part comprises, the actual material of his art. The 'arts' of, e.g., the strategist, the plumber, the philosopher, the physicist, are no doubt, like the art of the poet, conditioned by and reflective of the particular cultural complex to which their practitioners belong, but neither of these four arts, *with respect to their several causes*, can be said to be occupied with the embodiment and expression of the mythus and deposits comprising that cultural complex. Whereas the art of poetry, even in our present civilizational phase, even in our hyper-Alexandrian and megalopolitan situation, is, in some senses, still so occupied.

T. Gilby, in *Barbara Celarent*, writes 'The formal cause is the specific factor that we seek to capture, the mind is a hunter of forms, *venator formarum*'.

This, I suppose, applies to the 'specific factor' that the art of plumbing has as its formal cause, no less than to that which the art of poetry has. But the particular quarry that the mind of the poet seeks to capture is a very elusive beast indeed. Perhaps we can say that the country to be hunted, the habitat of that quarry, where the 'forms' lurk that he's after, will be found to be part of vast, densely wooded, inherited and entailed domains. It is in that 'sacred wood' that the spoor of those 'forms' is to be tracked. The 'specific factor' to be captured will be pungent with the smell of, asperged with the dew of, those thickets. The *venator poeta* cannot escape that tangled brake. It is within such a topography that he will feel forward, from a check to a find, from a find to a view, from a view to a possible kill: in the morning certainly, but also in the lengthening shadows.

Or, to leave analogy and to speak plain: I believe that there is, in the principle that informs the poetic art, a something which cannot be disengaged from the mythus, deposits, *matière*, ethos, whole *res* of which the poet is himself a product.

My guess is that we cannot answer the question 'What is poetry?' (meaning, What is the nature of poetry?) without some involvement in this mythus, deposit, etc.

We know—it goes without saying—that the question 'What is the material of poetry?' cannot be answered without some mention of these same deposits.

We know also, and even more certainly, that this applies to the question 'By what means or agency is poetry?' For one of the efficient causes of which the effect called poetry is a dependant involves the employment of a particular language or languages, and involves that employment at an especially heightened tension. The means or agent is a veritable torcular, squeezing every drain of evocation from the word-forms of that language or languages. And that involves a bagful of mythus before you've said Jack Robinson—or immediately after.

My contention is that all this holds whether the poet practises his art in some 'bardic' capacity and as a person of defined duties and recognized status in an early and simple phase of a culture (the 'morning' in the analogy employed above) or whether he happens to be a person who, for reasons of one sort or another, 'writes poetry' in a late and complex phase of a phenomenally complex civilization (the 'lengthening shadows' in the analogy) the many amenities of which you and I now enjoy.

We are not here considering the advantages or disadvantages to the art of poetry in these two totally other situations. We are noting only that in the latter situation the causes are *still* linked with the deposits.

We are, in our society of today, very far removed from those culture-phases where the poet was explicitly and by profession the custodian, rememberer, embodier and voice of the mythus, etc., of some contained group of families, or of a tribe, nation, people, cult. But we can, perhaps, diagnose something that appears as a constant in poetry by the following consideration:

When rulers seek to impose a new order upon any such group belonging to one or other of those more primitive culture-phases, it is necessary for those rulers to take into account the influence of the poets as recalling something loved and as embodying an ethos inimical to the imposition of that new order. Whether the policy adopted is one of suppression or of some kind of patronage, a recognition of possible danger dictates the policy in either case. Leaving aside such political considerations as may cause such recognition under such circumstances, we may still recognize the 'dangerous' element. Poetry is to be diagnosed as 'dangerous' because it evokes and recalls, is a kind of *anamnesis* of, i.e. is an effective recalling of, something loved. In that sense it is inevitably 'propaganda', in that any real formal expression propagands the reality which caused those forms and their content to be. There are also to be considered the contingent and more remote associations which those forms and their content may evoke. There is a sense in which *Barbara Allen* is many times more 'propagandist' than *Rule Britannia*. The more real the thing, the more it will confound their politics. If the dog-rose moves something in the Englishman at a deeper level than the Union Flag it is not only because of the fragile and peculiar beauty of that flower, but also because the poetry of England, drawing upon the intrinsic qualities of the familiar and common June rose, has, by the single image of a rose, managed to recall and evoke, for the English, a June-England association. The first concept being altogether and undeniably lovely, the other also must be lovely! A very satisfactory conclusion. The magic works. But it might prove most adverse magic to an opponent of the thing, idea or complex of sentiments which the word 'England' is patient of comprising.

The problems that confront the poet, as poet, in any given cultural or civilizational phase, no matter what his subjective attitude toward those problems, and though they concern only such elusive matters as the validity of a word, are themselves as objective as is the development of the aero-engine, the fact that my great-uncle William served in the ranks in the Crimea, that the tree outside the window happens to be an acacia, that field-archaeology has changed some of the accents of, e.g., Biblical criticism, that an extension of state-control characterizes the period in which we now live, or that something analogous to that extension is remarked by students of the period of Valens and Valentinian, and that like effects may possibly have like causes.

The poet is born into a given historic situation and it follows that his problems—i.e. his problems as a poet—will be what might be called 'situational problems'.

If, owing to a complex of causes, sable-hair brushes, chinese white and hot-pressed water-colour paper went off the market, you would, if you were a user of such commo-

dities, be faced with a situational problem of a very awkward
but fundamentally material sort. Whatever the consolation
of philosophy, no attitude of mind would bring back to your
workroom the required commodities which the market no
longer provided. You would willy-nilly suffer an inconvenience. The effect of that inconvenience *might* be most salutary, might occasion in you a most unsuspected inventiveness.
Well, the situational problem which concerns us here is of an
equally objective nature, but so far from affecting only the
materials of one particular kind of artist, it affects man-the-
artist as such, and affects him not at one peripheral point,
but crucially. Nevertheless, as with the inconvenienced
water-colourist, the 'inconveniences' of our situation may
turn out to be, in some respects and for some, 'most
salutary'. Indeed there is not wanting evidence that such is
the case. And so it is that the present situation presents its
own particular difficulties with regard to signs in general and
the concept of sign.

The whole complex of these difficulties is primarily felt
by the sign-maker, the artist, because for him it is an immediate, day by day, factual problem. He has, somehow or other,
to lift up valid signs; that is his specific task.

In practice one of his main problems, one of the matters
upon which his judgment is exercised ('The virtue of art is
to judge') concerns the validity and availability of his images.
It is precisely this validity and availability that constitutes his
greatest problem in the present culture-situation.

If the poet writes 'wood' what are the chances that the
Wood of the Cross will be evoked? Should the answer be
'None', then it would seem that an impoverishment of some
sort would have to be admitted. It would mean that that
particular word could no longer be used with confidence to
implement, to call up or to set in motion a whole world of
content belonging in a special sense to the mythus of a

particular culture and of concepts and realities belonging to mankind as such. This would be true irrespective of our beliefs or disbeliefs. It would remain true even if we were of the opinion that it was high time that the word 'wood' should be dissociated from the mythus and concepts indicated. The arts abhor any loppings off of meanings or emptyings out, any lessening of the totality of connotation, any loss of recession and thickness through.

If the painter makes visual forms, the content of which is chairs or chair-ishness, what are the chances that those who regard his painting will run to meet him with the notions 'seat', 'throne' 'session', *cathedra*', 'Scone', 'on-the-right-hand-of-the-Father', in mind? If this haphazard list is, in some of its accidents, yours and mine, it nevertheless serves, *mutatis mutandis*, for Peloponnesians and for Polynesians too.

It is axiomatic that the function of the artist is to make things *sub specie aeternitatis*.

'He said "What's Time? Leave Now for dogs and apes!
    Man has For ever".'

True, but the works of man, unless they are of 'now' and of 'this place', can have no 'for ever'.

The poet may feel something with regard to Penda the Mercian and nothing with regard to Darius the Mede. In itself that is a limitation, it might be regarded as a disproportion; no matter, there is no help—he must work within the limits of his love. There must be no mugging-up, no 'ought to know' or 'try to feel'; for only what is actually loved and known can be seen *sub specie aeternitatis*. The muse herself is adamant about this: she is indifferent to what the poet may wish he could feel, she cares only for what he in fact feels. In this she differs totally from her sister, the 'Queen of the Moral Virtues', who, fortunately for us, is concerned only with our will and intention.

This applies to poets, artefacturers of *opera* of any sort, at

[24]

any period of human history. But as I see it, we are today so situated that it is pertinent to ask: What for us *is* patient of being 'actually loved and known', where for us is 'this place', where do we seek or find what is 'ours', what *is* available, what *is* valid as material for our effective signs?

Normally we should not have far to seek: the flowers for the muse's garland would be gathered from the ancestral burial-mound—always and inevitably fecund ground, yielding perennial and familiar blossoms, watered and, maybe, potted, perhaps 'improved', by ourselves. It becomes more difficult when the bulldozers have all but obliterated the mounds, when all that is left of the potting-sheds are the disused hypocausts, and when where was this site and were these foci there is *terra informis*.

To what degree, for instance, is it possible for the 'name' to evoke the 'local habitation' long since gone? I do not raise these questions in order to answer them, for I do not know what the answers may be, but I raise them in order to indicate some of the dilemmas which have been present with me all the time.

When I was a child there was still in vogue the Victorian catch-question 'When is a door not a door?' Today I find that question has gathered to itself unexpected meaning. It has become the keynote of a so to say auto-catechism: When is a door not a door? When is a sign not a sign? When is what was valid no longer valid?

Such questions and attempts to answer them are in part reflected in the preoccupation with the 'abstract' in the visual arts. This preoccupation, whether mistaken or rewarding, is neither whim nor accident but is determined by historic causes affecting all this whole business of sign and what is signified, now-ness and place-ness and loves and validities of many sorts and kinds.

What goes for tinker goes for tailor; and it is worth

[25]

noting, for again it is not accidental, that the man who was super-sensitive to the unique and specific possibilities and demands of his own art, should have shown in his attitude toward that art and in that art itself, how analogous are some of the problems that the muse sets for the writer and those she sets for the painter. And further that this artist, while pre-eminently 'contemporary' and indeed 'of the future', was also of all artists the most of site and place. And as for 'the past', as for 'history', it was from the ancestral mound that he fetched his best garlands and Clio ran with him a lot of the way—if under the name of Brigit. So that although most authentically the bard of the shapeless cosmopolis and of the megalopolitan diaspora, he could say

'Come ant daunce wyt me
In Irelaunde'.

In taking Joyce to illustrate the problem I do so because any problem inherent in the arts today, and in particular in that of writing, is illuminated by so doing. Quite irrespective of whether we approve or deprecate his matter or his form or both, Joyce was centrally occupied with the formal problems of art, as exemplified in a particular art and in his own very particular deployment of that art. It is just such *kinds* of artist who alone illustrate the artistic dilemmas of any age. Hopkins, 'as one born out of due time', but before his time (yet how very much *of* his time!), was just such another. And we know how he, Manley Hopkins, stands over so many later artists, saying, in the words of another and pre-eminent living artist,

'And I Tiresias have foresuffered all'.

And Browning too might well have his say and continue the quotation,

'Enacted on this same divan or bed'.

That bed may indeed seem procrustean, for the artist may be stretched upon it

'Dead from the waist down'
and it is on such a couch that the muse exacts and interro-
gates, subsequent to
'The fine delight that fathers thought'.

To take an example from a visual art: Though our presiding
spirit were akin to that which presided over the illustrative
charm of Beatrix Potter, we should be more than foolish
to close our eyes to the existence of Pablo Picasso, because
our problems as a visual artist would be bound in some way or
other, to some degree or other, to involve matters over
which that Spanish Hercules has laboured in more than
twelve modes. Behind his untiring inventiveness there is the
desire to uncover a valid sign. And that desire is, as I have
said, incumbent upon all who practise an art.

A rhyme I associate with St Thomas More (but perhaps it
is not his) runs
'The cook that doth to painting fall
I ween he shall prove a fool'.
In practice maybe—it all depends. But in idea he will not be
proved so foolish as the painter who thinks cookery not
subject to the same demands of the muse as is painting or any
making that contrives things patient of being 'set up to the
gods'.

The foregoing considerations may appear to lack continu-
ity and to run tangent, but they will perhaps indicate something of my attitude toward human works of all sorts and are
thus not out of place in an introduction to this attempted
sort of work of my own.

I call what I have written *The Anathemata*. (The dictionary
puts the accent on the *third* syllable in contradistinction to
'anathemas'.)

It came to have this title in the following way: I knew that
in antiquity the Greek word *anathema* (spelt with an epsilon)
meant (firstly) something holy but that in the N.T. it is

restricted to the opposite sense. While this duality exactly fitted my requirements, the English word 'anathemas', because referring only to that opposite sense, was of no use to me. I recalled, however, that there was the other English plural, 'anathemata', meaning devoted things, and used by some English writers down the centuries, thus preserving in our language the ancient and beneficent meaning; for 'anathemata' comes from *anathema* spelt with an eta, of which the epsilon form is a variant.

It might be said that 'anathemata' precludes 'anathemas' no less than *vice versa*, but considering that the former carries us back to a beneficent original, and the latter only to a particular meaning of a variant of that original, I decided that 'anathemata' would serve my double purpose, even if it did so only by means of a pun.

Subsequent to deciding upon this title, I noted that in a reference to St John Chrysostom it was said that he described the word as 'things . . . laid up from other things'. And again that in Homer it refers only to delightful things and to ornaments. And further, that it is a word having certain affinities with *agalma*, meaning what is glorious, and so used of statue, image, figure. (Hence our word figure-stone, agalmatolite, called also pagodite because the sacred images or pagodas of Asia are carved in it.) And again in the gospel, after narrating the incident of the widow's mite, St Luke speaks of the onlookers who admired the 'goodly stones and gifts' that embellished the temple and he uses the word 'anathemata' of those gifts. And in the middle of the last century, an author, commenting on ancient votive offerings—figurines of animals—writes of 'such anathemata being offered by the poor'.

So I mean by my title as much as it can be made to mean, or can evoke or suggest, however obliquely: the blessed things that have taken on what is cursed and the profane

[28]

things that somehow are redeemed: the delights and also the 'ornaments', both in the primary sense of gear and para- phernalia and in the sense of what simply adorns; the donated and votive things, the things dedicated after whatever fashion, the things in some sense made separate, being 'laid up from other things'; things, or some aspect of them, that partake of the extra-utile and of the gratuitous; things that are the signs of something other, together with those signs that not only have the nature of a sign, but are themselves, under some mode, what they signify. Things set up, lifted up, or in whatever manner made over to the gods.

But here I shall have to recall an ancient distinction as it very much concerns, and is mixed up with, what I include under anathemata.

It is spoken of under the terms *prudentia* and *ars*. With regard to the latter, the 'virtue of art', a compact or ship- shape passage occurs in a recent book.[1] This passage con- cludes thus: 'The emphasis is on the thing to be done, not, as in the moral virtues, on our personal dispositions in doing it.' The one is concerned only for our intentions and dis- positions, and the other only for the formal dispositions that comprise an artefact. One cares for us and our final condition, the other for the work and *its* final condition. Our final con- dition or last end is not yet, whereas our artefacts have their completion now or never. For which reason, while Pru- dentia is exercised about our intentions, Ars is concerned with the shape of a finished article. She *cannot*, as the other *must*, wait till the Judgment.

---

[1] A book from which I have already quoted, by Thomas Gilby, O.P.
The distinction compactly put by Fr Gilby in this passage has indeed been expressed and many of its implications dwelt upon by my friend the late Mr Eric Gill; and I should like to take this opportunity of acknowledging my in- debtedness to those fruitful conversations with Mr Gill in years gone by, re- garding this business of man-the-artist. For he possessed, in conversation, a Socratic quality, which, even in disagreement, tended to clarification.

PREFACE

The distinction could hardly be greater in all respects—
that is what makes the analogies particularly significant. For
it emerges that both are concerned with the proper integration and perfection of a shape, in the one case that of persons
and in the other of perishable things. Both then are concerned
with what is patient of being 'devoted', 'laid up from other
things', 'consecrated to divine use', made anathemata in
some sense or other.

So that at one end of the scale or Jacob's ladder or song of
degrees, we can include, in respect of things offered, those
differing coloured marks or spots that boys chalk carefully
on their whipping-tops,[1] which, when they whip the top,
take on definity and form and appear as revolving circles of
rainbow hue. (And if this is not a gift to the muse, then I do
not know what is, and a falsity pervades my suppositions and
analogies throughout.)

At the other end we can include that which comprises
anathemata in *every possible* sense, offerings of both persons
and things, including those things over which the minister
is directed to say '. . . bless, ascribe to, ratify, make reasonable and acceptable'.[2]

We note that he is not directed to say those words with
reference to grapes and wheat,[3] but with reference to things

---

[1] Or did so forty or fifty years back.

[2] The actual form now in use is: '. . . *benedictam, adscriptam, ratam, rationabilem, acceptabilemque facere digneris*' and is part of the oblational prayers in the
Roman mass. As it stands in its Latin form it is only of the fourth century.
It is, however, said by liturgical scholars to link with forms in use in the Greek-
speaking Roman church about the beginning of the third century; a date as
near to St John or to 'Boadicea' as are you and I to William Blake or Maréchal
Ney.

[3] I seem to recall a passage in *The Shape of the Liturgy* (Dix) where the author,
referring to the words 'these thy creatures of bread and wine' in the *Book of
Common Prayer*, rightly says (as far as I can remember) that these words suggest
that bread and wine are simply fruits of the earth, whereas this is not strictly so.
At all events that is the distinction which I wish to emphasize here. It is one
which I think has very important implications and corollaries.

which have already passed under the jurisdiction of the muse, being themselves quasi-artefacts, made according to a *recta ratio* and involving the operation of several arts, as that of the mill, the kneading-board, the oven, the *torcular*, the vat.

So that, leaving aside much else, we could not have the bare and absolute essentials wherewith to obey the command 'Do this for a recalling[1] of me', without artefacture. And where artefacture is there is the muse, and those cannot escape her presence who with whatever intention employ the signs of wine and bread. Something has to be made by us before it can become for us his sign who made us. This point he settled in the upper room. No artefacture no Christian religion.[2] Thus far what goes for Mass-house goes for Meeting-house.[3] The muse then is with us all the way—she that has music wherever she goes.

This leads direct to a further point. I have already referred to what this writing 'is about'; but I now wish to add something rather more particularized and somewhat difficult to say.

In a sense the fragments that compose this book are about, or around and about, matters of all sorts which, by a kind of quasi-free association, are apt to stir in my mind at any time and as often as not 'in the time of the Mass'. The mental associations, liaisons, meanderings to and fro, 'ambivalences', asides, sprawl of the pattern, if pattern there is—these thought-trains (or, some might reasonably say, trains of distraction and inadvertence) have been as often as not initially set in motion, shunted or buffered into near sidings or off to far destinations, by some action or word, something seen or

---

[1] See note 1 to page 205 of text with regard to 'recalling' in this connection.

[2] Unless of course we regarded that religion as being *exclusively* concerned with an attitude of mind or state of soul.

[3] Except in some few denominations, e.g. the Society of Friends. Not that these escape either; for they employ forms of some kind and a genuine and very decent procedure. And where there is order and sensitivity to the conserving of a form, there is the muse.

[31]

heard, during the liturgy. The speed of light, they say, is very rapid—but it is nothing to the agility of thought and its ability to twist and double on its tracks, penetrate recesses and generally nose about. You can go around the world and back again, in and out the meanders, down the history-paths, survey *religio* and *superstitio*, call back many yesterdays, but yesterday week ago, or long, long ago, note Miss Weston's last year's Lutetian trimmings and the Roman laticlave on the deacon's Dalmatian tunic, and a lot besides, during those few seconds taken by the presbyter to move from the Epistle to the Gospel side, or while he leans to kiss the board or stone (where are the tokens of the departed) or when he turns to incite the living *plebs* to assist him.

But if the twists and turns that comprise thought are quicker than light, the action of making anything—any artefact or work of any sort—from those thoughts, is, as the tag says, longer.

The mote of dust or small insect seen for an instant in a bend or pale of light, may remind us of the bird that winged swiftly through the lighted mote-hall, and that I suppose cannot but remind us of the northern Witan and that may recall the city of York and that again Canterbury and that the 'blisful briddes', and that Tabard Street, E.C.1, and that London Bridge, and that the South Bank and its present abstract artefacts, and that again Battersea, and that the forcing of the river at the Claudian invasion, and that the 'Battersea shield', and that that other abstract art of the La Tène Celts in the British Museum in Bloomsbury, W.C.1.

This much and much more can be 'thought of' in a second or so. But suppose you had to make the actual journey by London Transport and British Railways, starting from the station down the road (Harrow Met.), keeping strictly to the order of your mental itinerary. It would take you not seconds but many, many hours; I should want some days and a long rest.

Now making a work is not thinking thoughts but accomplishing an actual journey. There are the same tediums: strugglings with awkward shapes that won't fit into the bag, the same mislayings, as of tickets, the missings of connections, the long waits, the misdirections, the packing of this that you don't need and the forgetting of that which you do, and all such botherations, not to speak of more serious mishaps. Until in the end you may perhaps wish you had never observed that mote of dust in the beam from the clerestory light that set you willy-nilly on your journey. You might have been better occupied. You well might. It is not without many such misgivings that I write this introduction to the meanderings that comprise this book.

What I have written has no plan, or at least is not planned. If it has a shape it is chiefly that it returns to its beginning. It has themes and a theme even if it wanders far. If it has a unity it is that what goes before conditions what comes after and *vice versa*. Rather as in a longish conversation between two friends, where one thing leads to another; but should a third party hear fragments of it, he might not know how the talk had passed from the cultivation of cabbages to Melchizedek, king of Salem. Though indeed he might guess.

Which means, I fear, that you won't make much sense of one bit unless you read the lot.

My intention has not been to 'edify' (in the secondary but accepted and customary sense of that word), nor, I think, to persuade, but there is indeed an intention to 'uncover'; which is what a 'mystery' does, for though at root 'mystery' implies a closing, all 'mysteries' are meant to disclose, to show forth something. So that in one sense it *is* meant to 'edify', i.e. 'to set up'. Otherwise my intentions would not sort very well with the title of my book, *The Anathemata*, 'the things set up, etc.'

Most of all, perhaps, I could wish of my 'mystery',

[33]

misterium or *ministerium*, that it should give some kind of
'pleasure', for I believe in Poussin's dictum: 'The goal of
painting is delight', and as I have already said, it is one of my
few convictions that what goes for one art goes for all of
'em, in some sense or other.

To reinforce something already touched upon: I regard my
book more as a series of fragments, fragmented bits, chance
scraps really, of records of things, vestiges of sorts and kinds
of *disciplinae*[1], that have come my way by this channel or
that influence. Pieces of stuffs that happen to mean something to me and which I see as perhaps making a kind of coat
of many colours, such as belonged to 'that dreamer' in the
Hebrew myth.[2] Things to which I would give a related
form, just as one does in painting a picture. You use the
things that are yours to use because they happen to be lying
about the place or site or lying within the orbit of your
'tradition'. It is very desirable in the arts to know the meaning of the word ex-orbitant, or there is pastiche or worse.

Of course, in any case, there may well be pastiche, padding,
things not gestant and superficialities of all sorts; but all this
is inevitable if you get outside what I believe Blake called the
artist's horizon. I have tried to keep inside it. Necessarily

---

[1] I use the word *disciplinae* here because I can't think of an English word
which covers what I intend: the various modes and traditions of doing this or
that, from bowling a hoop to engraving on copper; from 'Kiss in the Ring' to
serving at Mass; from forming fours (or threes) to Rolle of Hampole's *Form of
Perfect Living*; from Rugby Union Rules to the rules that governed court etiquette in the Welsh medieval codes; from the mixing of water-colours to the
mixing of pig-food; from mending the fire to mending the fire-step; from the
making of blackbird pie to the making of a king; from the immemorial nursery
methods of reminding children that they are not laws to themselves to the
three extinguishings of the lighted flax that at his coronation remind the
Pontiff Maximus of much the same truth, together with the words, which at
each extinguishing they say to him: *Sancte Pater, sic transit gloria mundi*. For in
a sense all *disciplinae* are warnings 'This is the way to make the thing, that way
won't do at all'.

[2] 'Myth', see note to page 40 below.

within that 'horizon' you will find material of which it could
be said

> '. . . in scole is gret altercacioun
> In this matere, and gret disputision'

and, although it is absolutely incumbent upon the artist to
use this disputed 'matere', he may be the least qualified to
discuss it, nor is it his business, *qua* artist. He has not infre-
quently to say, quoting from the same clear source of
Englishness,

> 'Those been the cokkes wordes and not myne'.

Rather than being a seer or endowed with the gift of pro-
phecy he is something of a vicar whose job is legatine—a
kind of Servus Servorum to deliver what has been delivered
to him, who can neither add to nor take from the deposits.
It is not that that we mean by 'originality'. There is only one
tale to tell even though the telling is patient of endless
development and ingenuity and can take on a million variant
forms. I imagine something of this sort to be implicit in what
Picasso is reported as saying: 'I do not seek, I find'.

I intend what I have written to be said. While marks of
punctuation, breaks of line, lengths of line, grouping of
words or sentences and variations of spacing are visual con-
trivances they have here an aural and oral intention. You
can't get the intended meaning unless you hear the sound and
you can't get the sound unless you observe the score; and
pause-marks on a score are of particular importance. Lastly,
it is meant to be said with deliberation—slowly as opposed
to quickly—but 'with deliberation' is the best rubric for
each page, each sentence, each word.

I would especially emphasize this point, for what I have
written will certainly lose half what I intend, indeed, it will
fail altogether, unless the advice 'with deliberation' is
heeded. Each word is meant to do its own work, but each
word cannot do its work unless it is given due attention. It

was written to be read in that way. And, as I say above, the spacings are of functional importance; they are not there to make the page look attractive—though it would be a good thing should that result also.

'Old Johnny Faírplay all the way from Bómbay . . . the more you put down the more you pick up . . . páy the man his móney.'

In the 1914-18 army there used to be played a proscribed game of chance, and a reiterated form of words, a kind of liturgic refrain heard from among a huddle of players, included the words above quoted.[1] It was part of the ritual of the game and might involve a few centimes or a substantial number of francs; little or much. It seems to me only decent that those should be paid acknowledgment who by some work of theirs have, however obliquely, aided us to make our artefacts. Of course there is the other reflection which 1914-18 painfully recalls, 'No names, no pack-drill', but I think we'll chance it.

First, perhaps, I should mention Mr Christopher Dawson, to whose writings and conversation I feel especially indebted. Then there is Mr W. F. Jackson Knight whose particular *numen* or sprite is something of an Ariadne, who pays out more than one length of thread. He, too, would lighten the kitty, had he his due. As it is impossible to write down anything like a complete, or even a representative, list of living or recently living authors to whom I stand indebted in little or much, I shall give fifty names which shall be chosen as they happen to come to mind as I now write: Maurice de la Taille, Oswald Spengler, Jacques Maritain, James Frazer, Jessie Weston, Christopher and Jacquetta

---

[1] The middle fragment may be inaccurate as it is thirty-four years since I last heard it.

Hawkes, Jane Harrison, Gilbert Sheldon, Martin D'Arcy, Louis Duchesne, Louis Gougaud, Gregory Dix, C. H. Cochrane, T. C. Lethbridge, John Edward Lloyd, Ifor Williams, W. F. Grimes, T. Gwynne Jones, A. H. Williams, W. J. Gruffydd, Henry Lewis, T. D. Kendrick, Henri Hubert, Henri Pirenne, R. G. Collingwood with J. N. L. Myres, H. Stuart Jones, Rachel Levy, Cecile O'Rahilly, Laura Keeler, H. M. Chadwick, Margaret Deansley, J. R. R. Tolkien, W. R. Lethaby, S. E. Winbolt, Benjamin Farrington, A. T. Mahan, E. G. R. Taylor, Géza Róheim, C. C. Martindale, Friedrich von Hügel, A. W. F. Blunt, E. C. Blackman, K. E. Kirk, T. Neville George with Bernard Smith, Dora Ware with Betty Beatty, E. K. Chambers, F. M. Powicke, J. Livingstone Lowes, O. G. S. Crawford, A. W. Wade Evans, Gordon Home, A. M. Hocart, but I'm afraid I've exceeded the fifty and must stop.

Some on this brief, arbitrary and very chancy list are recalled perhaps on account of a few informative diagrams or clarifying passages. Some have been deliberately consulted to check up on a half-remembered matter, others have been influential in a more pervasive way. Some are gratefully remembered for a popular, modest, concise, elementary textbook such as *A Short Dictionary of Architecture including some Common Building Terms* by Ware and Beatty. Others for crucial and great works such as Père de la Taille's thesis on the relationship of what was done in the Supper-room with what was done on the Hill and the further relationship of these doings with what is done in the Mass.[1]

---

[1] I have not read, nor am I able to read, the original work in Latin, entitled *Mysterium Fidei*; but an outline of his thesis appeared in English by de la Taille in 1934 and it is to this that I refer. There was also *The Mass and the Redemption* by Fr D'Arcy, again elucidating in English the same theme.

Since first hearing of this thesis in *c*. 1923, I was drawn to what seemed, to my untrained mind, its integration and creativity, and it seemed to illumine things outside its immediate theological context.

Others are recalled for bringing a less tired vision to bear on this matter or that, such as the late Gilbert Sheldon in *The Transition from Roman Britain to Christian England*. Others again for works of natural science or of specialist research, such as the contributions of B. Smith and T. N. George to the *British Regional Geology* series, or E. G. R. Taylor's articles on classical and medieval seafaring that she contributed to *The Journal of the Institute of Navigation*, edited by Mr M. W. Richey; or the monograph by Laura Keeler of the University of California, entitled *Geoffrey of Monmouth and the Late Latin Chroniclers*.

I have not included here any of those whose influence I associate chiefly with the 'form' of what I have written. It is confined to those whose works have had a bearing on the 'content' only, or principally so. The intention here is to acknowledge information and data.

There are, however, many others to whom I may be as, or more, indebted. Who should say how much may be owing to a small textbook on botany; a manual of seamanship; various items in the magazine *Wales* edited by Mr Keidrych Rhys; a guide to the Isle of Wight; a child's picture-book of prehistoric fauna; a guide-book to the parish church of Cilcain, Flintshire, by a local antiquary, 1912; a glossy 1949 bookstall purchase on the pontifex Isambard Kingdom Brunel; a brochure on the composition and permanence of colours; a pamphlet on the prevention of collisions at sea; a paper read before a London conference of psychologists; the text of a guide to a collection of Welsh samplers and embroideries; a catalogue of English china or plate; a neglected directive from Rome on the use of the Chant; a reference in *The Times* to the cry of a bittern in Norfolk, or to the bloom on a thorn-bush in Herefordshire, or to an Homeric find on Karatepe ridge?

Then there are the conversations that have had a direct and

immediate bearing of some kind. Among many such I call to
mind talks with the late Eric Burrows, and with Richard
Kehoe and Bernard Wall.

I thank all those many old or more recent friends who have
assisted me in many various ways and by kindnesses, toler-
ances and understandings of all sorts.

As in writing the preface to *In Parenthesis* fourteen years
ago, I must again especially thank my friend Mr Harman
Grisewood for his encouragement and for his critical assist-
ance whenever it was sought, over the form here or the
content there.

Others of whose help I am *particularly* sensible, I fear I
shall have to leave unnamed, rather than omit any. These
include some of my nearest friends, and I am grateful to
them all.[1]

I have already given a random list of some few contemporary 'authorities' to whom I know myself indebted, but
there are the more formidable and more forming creditors
of the past. I shall not attempt to make a list of them,
whether they were living in the world of Kipling's khaki
limes, or in the world of R. T. McMullen (who circum-
navigated the Island in the Jubilee Year), or in the world of
Heinrich Schliemann (who digged nine sites down in Helen's
laughless rock) or in that of Cruikshank's Boz, or that of
Smith the lexicographer. Or in the period of 'poor Smart'
(for whom, Alleluia!), or of John Gay, or of Herbert of
Cherbury, or of Stow the Londoner, or of Adam of Usk, or
of Langland the Englishman, or of Duns the Scot and the
Angel from Aquin; or of those various Chrétiens who
French-polished the *matière de Bretagne* (confounding the
topography and playing Old Harry with the persons, for all

---

[1] Nor can I neglect to mention those doctors, necessarily unnamed, and
nurses who, by the practice of their arts, aided me to re-continue the practice of
mine.

the perfections of their art) or of Gerald the Welshman, or
of Anselm the I-talian. Then there are the basic things: the
early mixed racial deposits, the myth (mythus)[1] that is
specifically of this Island, and the Christian Liturgy, and the
Canon of Scripture, and the Classical deposits. I list these
four thus for mere convenience. Clearly they comprise in
our tradition a great complex of influences and interactions
which have conditioned us all. To say that one draws upon
such deposits does not imply erudition; it suggests only that
these form the *materia* that we *all* draw upon, whether we
know it or not, to this degree or that, in however roundabout
a way, whether we are lettered or illiterate, Christian or
post-Christian, or anti-Christian.

Then there are the living, dying, or dead traditions in
which one has oneself participated or heard of with one's
own ears from one's own parents or near relatives or immediate forebears. These things received in childhood are of
course fragments or concomitants only of the whole above-
mentioned complex. I am thinking only of the means whereby
those concomitants and fragments reached me. I am speaking
of channels only, but of immediate channels and such as
condition all that passes through them, and which condition

---

[1] I prefer 'myth' to 'mythus', but owing to such sentences as 'She said she'd
got some fags, but it was a pure myth' the meaning of 'myth' is liable to misunderstanding even in the most serious connections.

Unfortunately *The Shorter Oxford English Dictionary* (1933) defines 'myth' as
'A purely fictitious narrative, etc.' Yet we sing in the Liturgy '*Teste David cum
Sibylla*' and clearly the Sibyl belongs to what, for the Christian Church, is an
extra-revelational body of tradition. But such bodies of tradition are not to be
described as 'purely fictitious', yet they are certainly properly described as
'myth'. I choose this example from among innumerable others, because of the accepted rule that the public prayer of an institution is a sure gauge to the mind
of the institution that employs that prayer. I don't mind the rather academic
'mythus' but I don't see why we should have the English form 'myth' perma-
nently separated from its primal innocence, from the Greek *mythos*, which, I
understand, means a word uttered, something told. Then we should rightly
speak of the myth of the Evangel, a myth devoid of the fictitious, an utterance
of the Word, a 'pure myth'.

[40]

also one's subsequent attitude to all the rest. These I judge to be of the most primary importance. It is through them that 'all the rest' is already half sensed long before it is known. If ever it is known. You smell a rat or two pretty early on.

It so happens that whereas I did drawings from five years onwards I was very stupid in learning to read and found it hard at nine and subsequently. On more than one occasion I recall paying my sister a penny to read to me. There was in those days a children's pink paper-covered series called Books for the Bairns and one of that series dealt with King Arthur's knights (including the story of the Knight of the Sparrow-hawk) and that was the book I most liked hearing read. And then *The Lays of Ancient Rome* became a favourite. I used to try to read, or rather turn over the pages of, Jewel's *Apology*, partly I think because that was in full calf, which I thought grand. Also there was Keble's *Christian Year* with illustrations by Johann Friedrich Overbeck.

Then my father sometimes read Bunyan aloud. Then there was the attempt to imitate the sounds when he sang *Mae hen wlad fy nhadau* or *Ar hyd y nos*. But without success. A failure which has pursued me. And then there were the reproductions of two or three thirteenth-century drawings of Welsh foot-soldiers in J. R. Green's *Short History of the English People*. These were a particular delight to me. And what lively drawings they in fact are. The draughtsman undoubtedly got the Welsh 'look'. [1]

---

[1] The originals are, I believe, in a collection called 'Liber A' in the Public Records Office. In the thirteenth century it was customary to give documents a marginal device for purposes of cataloguing, and for those dealing with Wales the official device was a Welsh bowman or a Welsh spearman. As far as I know these are among the very few visual representations of Welshmen from AD 400 to 1282 and after. There are just a few other indications, but very, very few. So that these drawings are of unusual interest. The lack of visual representation is one of the most distressing things about all matters touching the Welsh

It would seem that whether or no 'old friends are the best', they appear, in some ways, to be stayers.

It may be yesterday only that you heard of the significance of *The Epistle of Clement* and but a few years back that the other Clement's *Exhortation to the Greeks* was recommended to you by a perceptive cousin. But it was very many years ago that you wondered what Clement had to do with Danes. And it was much longer still ago that an aunt initiated you into 'Oranges and Lemons'. She may have been evasive when asked, 'Aunty, what's Clemens?' but she was handing down a traditional form and starting up in you a habit of 'recalling'. For names linger, especially when associated with some sort of *disciplina ludi*. They go into your word-hoard, whether or no you ever attempt to unlock it. No need to say anything further here of those channels, those creditors, for the book itself is meant to pay a farthing or two of that inescapable great debt.

I have a last point that I wish to get clear. Although in the notes to the text and in this apology I refer to or cite various authorities and sources, that does not mean that this book has any pretensions whatever of a didactic nature. I refer to those sources only to elucidate a background. As often as not I have no means of judging the relative accuracy of these data. I refer to them only as a traveller might, in making a song or story about a journey he had taken from his home through far places and back. He may have been impressed by the

---

past. There are innumerable references to clothes and arms in the written deposits, as in the *Gododdin* and in the Welsh Laws and in the vivid descriptions of Giraldus, but we have no visual counterpoint to any of this. We would like to know what Maelgwn Gwynedd or Hywel the Good *looked* like; in what did the cut of their coats differ from that of those worn by Chilperic or Henry the Fowler, their respective near contemporaries? A single drawing is more objective than whole pages of descriptive writing. So that we are greatly indebted to these thirteenth-century English clerks who sketched the appropriate marginal signs on the *Littera Wallie* and the *Scripta Wallie*.

clarity of a waterfall here, by the courage and beauty of the inhabitants there, or by the note of a bird elsewhere. And these phenomena would be deployed throughout his song as providing part of the content and affecting the form of that song. Such a person *might* choose to gloss what he was writing, or to break off from his narrative in order to tell his audience what the locals averred of those falling waters, or what the anthropologists had established with regard to the ancestry of those inhabitants, or how the ornithologists maintained that that bird-song was the song of no bird known to them. Such glosses might be made in order to explain some 'how' or 'why' of the relevant text.

The notes, because they so often concern the *sounds* of the words used in the text, and are thus immediately relevant to its *form*, are printed along with it, rather than at the back of the book. But this easy availability would be a disadvantage if it detracted attention from the work itself. So I ask the reader, *when actually engaged upon the text*, to consult these glosses mainly or only on points of pronunciation. For other purposes they should be read separately.

Words in Latin follow a 'modern' pronunciation: *c* and *g* hard, *ae* as *i* in wine. This rule is important as it affects the consonance and sometimes the rhyme. Exception may be made in quotations from the Liturgy where softenings would occur, but this affects a dozen words only throughout.

Lastly I wish to thank Ruth Winawer and Nest Cleverdon for kindly typing my MS with such care and efficiency.

Harrow-on-the-Hill
July 1951

DAVID JONES

IT WAS A DARK AND STORMY NIGHT, WE SAT BY THE CALCINED WALL; IT WAS SAID TO THE TALE-TELLER, TELL US A TALE, AND THE TALE RAN THUS: IT WAS A DARK AND STORMY NIGHT . . .

I

RITE AND FORE-TIME

PARENTIBVS
MEIS·ET·PRIOR
IBVSEORVM
ETOMNIBVS
INDIGENIS
OMNIS·CAN
DIDÆINSVLÆ
BRITTONVM
GENTIS

THE ANATHEMATA
TESTE DAVID CVM SIBYLLA

We already and first of all discern him making this thing other. His groping syntax, if we attend, already shapes:

ADSCRIPTAM, RATAM, RATIONABILEM . . .[1] and by pre-application and for *them*, under modes and patterns altogether theirs, the holy and venerable hands[2] lift up an efficacious sign.

These, at the sagging end and chapter's close, standing humbly before the tables spread, in the apsidal houses, who intend life:

> between the sterile ornaments
> under the pasteboard baldachins
> as, in the young-time, in the sap-years:
> between the living floriations
> under the leaping arches.

(Ossific, trussed with ferric rods, the failing numina of column and entablature, the genii of spire and triforium, like great rivals met when all is done, nod recognition across the cramped repeats of their dead selves.)

---

[1] See the Roman Mass, the Prayer of Consecration, beginning 'Which oblation do thou . . . ascribe to, ratify, make reasonable. . . .'
[2] Cf. the same, '. . . in sanctas ac venerabiles manus suas. . . .'

These rear-guard details in their quaint attire, heedless of incongruity, unconscious that the flanks are turned and all connecting files withdrawn or liquidated—that dead symbols litter to the base of the cult-stone, that the stem by the palled stone is thirsty, that the stream is very low.

> The utile infiltration nowhere held
> creeps vestibule
is already at the closed lattices,[1] is coming through each door.

The cult-man stands alone in Pellam's[2] land: more precariously than he knows he guards the *signa*: the pontifex among his house-treasures, (the twin-*urbes* his house is) he can fetch things new and old:[3] the tokens, the matrices, the institutes, the ancilia, the fertile ashes—the palladic foreshadowings: the things come down from heaven together with the kept memorials, the things lifted up and the venerated trinkets.

This man, so late in time, curiously surviving, shows courtesy to the objects when he moves among, handles or puts aside the name-bearing instruments, when he shows every day in his hand[4] the salted cake given for this *gens* to savour all the *gentes*.[5]

---

[1] Cf. the derivation of the word chancel, from *cancelli*, lattice bars.

[2] King Pellam in Malory's *Morte D'arthur* is lord of the Waste Lands and the lord of the Two Lands.

[3] Cf. 'Every scribe instructed in the kingdom of heaven is like to a man who is a householder, who bringeth forth out of his treasure new things and old.' See the Common of a Virgin Martyr, Mass 2, Gospel.

[4] Cf. Middle-English poem: *Of a rose a lovly rose* 'Every day it schewit in prystes hond'.

[5] *Mola salsa*, the cake of spelt and salt made by the Roman Vestals and used at the purification of sacrifices; and cf. Mark IX, 49-50, which indicates the same use of salt in Jewish rites.

Within the railed tumulus [1]
    he sings high and he sings low.

  In a low voice
      as one who speaks
where a few are, gathered in high-room
    and one, gone out.

  There's conspiracy here:
    Here is birthday and anniversary, if there's continuity
here, there's a new beginning.
  By intercalation of weeks
      (since the pigeons were unfledged
    and the lambs still young)
    they've adjusted the term
    till this appointed night
                  (Sherthursdaye bright) [2]

---

[1] 'tumulus' because the tumuli, the barrows on our downlands and hill-sites, were essentially burial places and because a Christian altar, by the requirements of Canon Law, and in observance of a use at least as old as the fourth century, should contain relics of the dead. Cf. at the beginning of Mass the priest kisses the altar, saying, '. . . by the merits of thy saints whose relics are here. . . .' and cf. the Offertory prayer *Suscipe sancta trinitas* in which the words occur 'and of these here' (*et istorum*). This prayer is very explicit; it says that the oblation is offered to the Trinity, in remembrance of the Passion, Resurrection and Ascension and in honour of the Theotokos, of certain named saints and those whose relics lie under the particular altar at which the Mass is being celebrated, together with all the saints departed.

[2] See *Le Morte d'Arthur*, xvii, 20, 'Everyman' edition; modernized spelling: 'the holy dish wherein I ate the lamb on Sher-Thursday'.

The textual authority on Malory's works, Professor Vinaver, gives 'on Estir Day' for Caxton's 'on sherthursdaye' and notes the latter as a corrupt variant. A French source is given as *le jour de Pasques*.

But as the words 'Thursday' and 'the holy dish' are, by gospel, rite, calendar and cultus, indissolubly connected, I regard Caxton's variant as most fortunate. Hence the use of 'sherthursdaye' here and in the title of Section 8 of this book.

the night that falls
when she's first at the full
after the vernal turn
when in the Ram he runs. [1]

By the two that follow Aquarius [2]
toiling the dry meander:
            through the byes
under the low porch
up the turning stair
to the high nave

            where the board is
to spread the board-cloth
under where the central staple is
for the ritual light.

In the high cave they prepare
            for guest to be the *hostia*.

---

[1] The conditions determining the exact time of the Passover were that the moon must be at the full, the vernal equinox past and the sun in Aries. The fixed date of the feast was the fourteenth day of the first month, Nisan; and if that date was due to fall before these conjunctions the necessary number of days were inserted into the calendar in order to postpone it. Subsidiary causes influencing this intercalation, such as the backwardness of the crops and the beasts, are also mentioned in the rabbinical writings. There was as yet no fixed calendar and adjustments were made each year on an empirical basis.

See Schürer, *Hist. of Jewish People*, Div. 1, Vol. II, Appendix. 'The Jewish and Macedonian months compared with the Julian calendar.' (Eng. Trans. Edtn. 1890.)

[2] Cf. the instructions given to Peter and John in the Passion according to Luke.

'As you go into the city there shall meet you a man carrying a pitcher of water: follow him into the house where he entereth in . . . And he will show you a large dining-room furnished: and there prepare.' (Trans. of Vulgate.)

The passage also partly reflects memories I have of walking in the lanes of Jerusalem, the excessive dryness and white dust, the low arched entries and stairs up into cool interior rooms.

They set the thwart-boards
and along:
    Two for the Gospel-makers[1]
    One for the other Son of Thunder
    One for the swordsman, at the right-board,[2] after;
to make him feel afloat. One for the man from Kerioth,[3]
seven for the rest in order.

They besom here and arrange this handy, tidy here, and
furbish with the green of the year the cross-beams and the
gleaming board.

    They make all shipshape
        for she must be trim
                dressed and gaudeous
    all Bristol-fashion here
    for:
        Who d'you think is Master of her?

In the prepared high-room
he implements inside time and late in time under forms in-
delibly marked by locale and incidence, deliberations made
out of time, before all oreogenesis

        on this hill
  at a time's turn
      not on any hill
  but on this hill.

---

[1] Cf. song, *Green grow the rashes O*
  'Four for the Gospel makers'.

Of the four evangelists, Matthew was present at the supper. John, one of the
two 'Sons of Thunder', was also present. Whether this was the author of the
Fourth Gospel has been much debated. Here the traditional identification is
taken for granted.

[2] 'the right-board'—starboard.

[3] Kerioth, a village of Judea from which Judas came, hence 'the Iscariot'.

[53]

1 'This is the Aristotelian theory of the Great Summer and the Great Winter, according to which the earth passes through a cycle of climatic change, each phase of which is linked with a corresponding change in the relative area of land and sea.' Dawson, *Age of the Gods*, 1929. The author goes on to explain that this Greek guess as to the cosmic rhythm is largely verified by modern physical science.

2 Cf. the layout of a *templum* (space), temple, camp, city, etc., with which the city on the seven hills is associated, and the connection between this and the prehistoric settlements on the marls of the Po Valley—hence called the Terramara (marl-earth) Culture. See page 81 below.

3 *Carneddau*, carn-neth-ei, neth as in nether, ei as in height, accent on middle syllable; thus rhyming with Volcae in the same line, and having some slight assonance with *Arthuri* below. *Carneddau* is the plural of *carnedd* a mound or cairn.

It was from *Volcae*, the name of a Celtic tribe, that the Teutonic word *Wealas*, 'the Welsh', derived. Just as the Romans got from the Illyrians the word 'Greeks' and applied it to all the Hellenes, so the Germans used the name of one Celtic tribe to designate other Celts. Later it meant 'foreigners' and was so used by the English of the Celts in this country, but only of those Celts who had formed part of the Roman world. The Anglo-Saxons did not call the Scots or the Picts *Wealas*, though these were equally foreigners and Celts. So that *Bret-Wealas*, Brit-Welsh, might be said to mean 'British-Roman foreigners'.

4 *Moel*, pronounce moil, hill.

5 'In Wales or in the March of Wales.' I write *Walliae* for 'of Wales', although in the thirteenth century document quoted, this genitive is spelt *Wallie*. But I wish it to be pronounced *Walliae*, ae as i in wine, thus rhyming with the immediately following word *ogofau* (caves) and having assonance with Owain, which rhymes with wine.

6 *Ogofau*, caves, og-ov-ei, ei as in height. Plutarch, in *Of the Failing Oracles*, says that Cronos sleeps in a cave in Britain; and in Welsh folk-tradition, both Arthur and Owain (Owen of the Red Hand, Yvain de Galles in Froissart) have been assimilated into this tradition of a sleeping hero who shall come again.

7 *Buarth Meibion Arthur*, bee-arrth mei-be-yon (ei as in height) arr-thur; 'The Enclosure of the Children of Arthur'. This name, and such names as 'The Stones of the Children of Arthur' and 'The Mound of the Children of Owen', occur as the local traditional names for various stone circles and burial-chambers in what comprised the Principality of Wales and the March of Wales.

8 The legend that gave a Trojan origin to the Britons made Camber, a supposed great-grandson of Aeneas, the eponym of Cambria. Cf. among the last tragic diplomatic exchanges between the lord Llywelyn ap Gruffydd, *princeps Wallie*, and Friar John, Archbishop Pecham, where appeal is made to this supposed Trojan origin; cf. also the phrase 'the dregs of the Trojans' quoted by Henry of Knyghton with reference to the dead lord Llywelyn. For the continued popularity of this theme, cf. *Henry V*, V, 2. *Pist.* Base Trojan thou shalt die. *Flu.* You say very true, scauld knave, when God's will is.

9 It was in a strategic key-position, on the mound of Hissarlik ('place of forts'), some three to four miles from the Dardanelles, about forty metres above sea-level, that Troy stood. Nine successive cities have occupied the site.

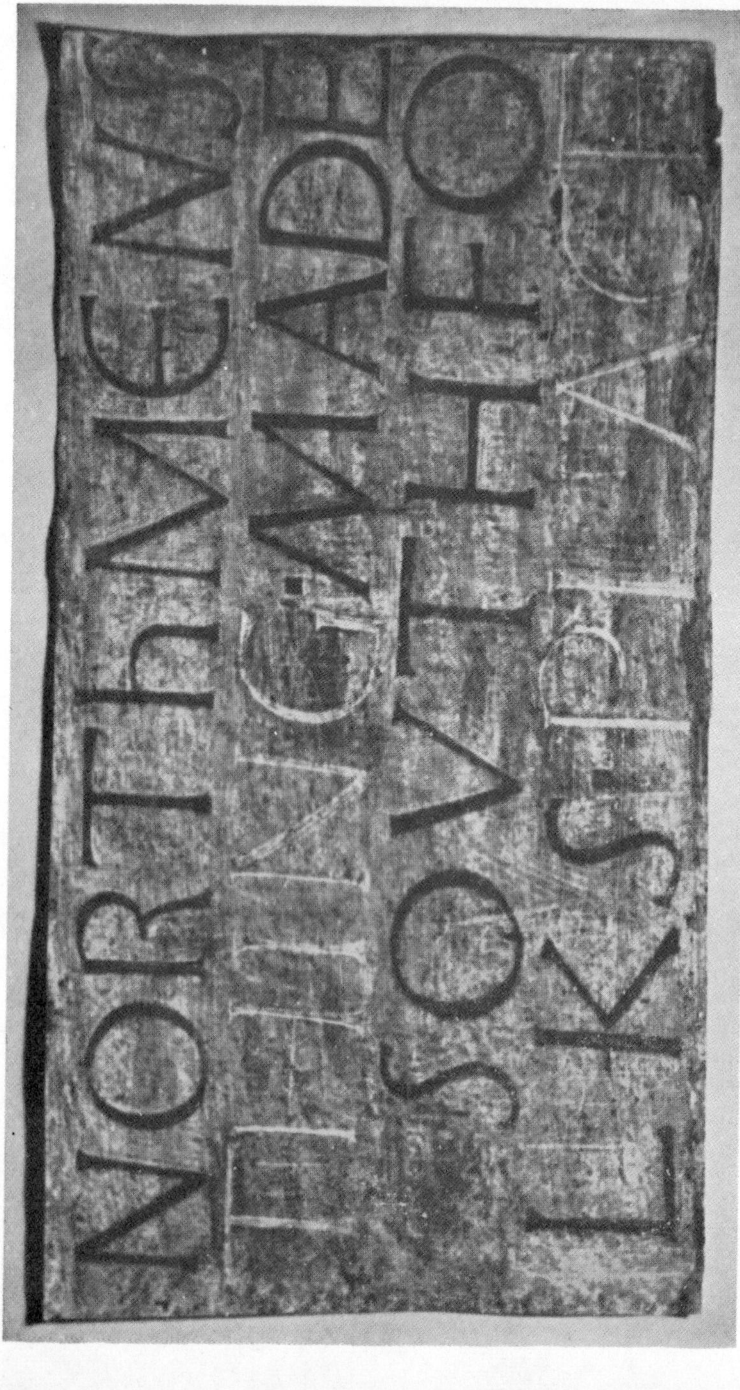

[On this unabiding rock
                    for one Great Summer
                         lifted up
                    by next Great Winter[1]
                         down
among the altitudes
with all help-heights
                    down
as low as Parnassus
                    (it's Ossa on Pelion now).
Seven templum'd montes
                    under terra-marl.[2]
Sinai under.
                    Where's Ark-hill?
Ask both the Idas.
And where:
                    West horse-hills?
                    Volcae-remnants' crag-*carneddau*?[3]
                    Moel[4] of the Mothers?
                    the many *colles Arthuri*?

All the efficacious asylums
in Wallia vel in Marchia Walliae,[5]
                    ogofau[6] of, that cavern for
                    Cronos, Owain, Arthur.
Terra Walliae!
                    Buarth Meibion Arthur![7]
                    Enclosure of the Children of Troy![8]

Nine-strata'd Hissarlik[9]
                    a but forty-metre height
yet archetype of sung-heights.

[55]

Crux-mound at the node
gammadion'd castle.
Within the laughless Megaron
   the margaron [1]
beyond echelon'd Skaian
   the stone
   the fonted water
   the fronded wood. [2]

Little Hissarlik
   least of acclivities
yet
   high as Hector the Wall
   high as Helen the Moon
who, being lifted up
   draw the West to them.

Hissarlik, traversed Hissarlik
   mother of forts
   hill of cries
small walled-height
   that but 750 marching paces would circuit [3]

---

[1] I am associating the rock called Agelastos Petra, 'the laughless rock', at pre-Hellenic Eleusis (where the modelled cult-object in its stone cist within the cleft of the rock, represented the female generative physiognomy) with the Megaron-type buildings on Troy-rock where Helen was the pearl-to-be-sought within the traversed and echeloned defences of the city. But apart from this association we can accurately describe the hall of Priam as 'laughless', and certainly Helen was a margaron of great price.

[2] Where Vergil (Aeneid II, 512-514) describes the palace of Priam he uses ancient material as to sacred tree and stone but puts them in a contemporary setting—a Roman *atrium*—so water is implied, for an atrium would have its sunk basin. By whatever means of fusion he hands down three of the permanent symbols for us to make use of.

[3] Helen's Troy seems to have been circular and about 200 yards in diameter —so about 628 yards in circumference (=753 military paces).

first revetted of anguish-heights[1]
                    matrix for West-*oppida*
                            for West-technic
                            for West-saga

down

                    under, sheet-darkt Hellespont?
                    pack for the Cyclades?
And where, from the potent flotsam, florid she breached,
with spume on her spear-flukes,[2] the great fluked mammals
blow? glaciation cones her own Thebes?[3] loess drifts Leo-
gate?

All *montes*
        with each dear made-height
et omnes colles
        down?
hautes eagle-heights under
low as Lambourn Down?
        As solitary tump, so massif?
Alp, as Bredon
        down?
obedient to the fiery stress
und icy counter-drag
        down, and

---

[1] Troy was one of the first walled cities. We can therefore take it as arche-
typal of all defended sites, and the persistence and integral position of the
story of Troy and of Helen in our Western tradition thus finds support in
modern scientific archaeology; while our civilization remains the word 'Troy'
will equate automatically with 'love and war'.

[2] When I wrote this I had an idea that in some presentation of the nativity
of the goddess, she is shown with a spear or fish-hook, but I can get no confirmation of this and therefore suppose I am mistaken. I will let it remain, because,
after all, a fish-spear is not inappropriate to her, whether as sea-goddess or
goddess of love.

[3] Aphrodite was patroness of the city of Thebes.

there shall be yet *more*
        storm-dark sea?[1]

Lord! what a morning yet may break
on this new-founded Oberland.]

At this unabiding Omphalos
        this other laughless rock
at the stone of division
        above the middle water-deeps[2]
at the turn of time
        not at any time, but
at this acceptable time.
From the year of
        the lord-out-of-Ur
about two millennia.
Two thousand lents again
        since the first barley mow.[3]

---

[1] Of the most extensive of all past glaciations—that of the Permo-Carboniferous age—it is said that the sheet-ice reached nearly as far as the Equator. I have no idea if at some remote geological time from now, there is any possibility of a similar glaciation. In the whole passage in square brackets I am merely employing such a possibility as a convenient allegory. There are freezings-up and convulsions of many kinds, there are 'ends' of all sorts of 'worlds', as we in our age have reason to understand. There are also new beginnings and freeings of the waters.

[2] The great rock over which the temple of Jerusalem was built was regarded not only as the navel of the world but as separating the waters of the abyss under the earth from the celestial waters.

[3] It is usually supposed that Abraham moved north-west up the Euphrates valley from 'Ur of the Chaldees' about 2,000 BC. The cultivation of grain had begun in Mesopotamia at least by 4,000 BC.

Twenty millennia (and what millennia more?)
Since he became
            man master-of-plastic. [1]

Who were his *gens*-men or had he no *Hausname* yet
no *nomen* for his *fecit*-mark
            the Master of the Venus?
whose man-hands god-handled the Willendorf stone
            before they unbound the last glaciation
for the Uhland Father to be-ribbon *die blaue Donau*
            with his Vanabride blue. [2]
O long before they lateen'd her Ister
or Romanitas manned her gender'd stream.

O Europa!
                        how long and long and long and
very long again, before you'll maze the waltz-forms in gay
Vindobona in the ramshackle last phases; or god-shape the
modal rhythms for nocturns in Melk in the young-time; [3] or
plot the Rhaetian limits in the Years of the City. [4]
            But already he's at it
the form-making proto-maker
busy at the fecund image of her.

---

[1] The first examples of visual art so far (1940) discovered date from about
20,000 BC. There is evidence of artefacture, of a sort, twenty thousand and
more years earlier still, e.g. flints and marked stones, but these are hardly
'visual art' in the accepted sense.

[2] In Northern myth, Uhland is the abode of the gods of the atmosphere, the
Luftraum. Vanabride is Freyja, a kind of Teutonic Venus. White cats draw her
car across the blue sky and her myth seems in part confused with that of Frigg
the wife of Odin. She is the most beautiful of the Vanir and half the departed
(who die bravely) are hers.

[3] The reference is to the Benedictine abbey of Melk, in Austria, which I am
told was one of the great centres of church music.

[4] Cf. the *Limes Raetiae*, which marked the limits of the civilized world in the
Danube district.

Chthonic? why yes
but mother of us.
Then it is these abundant *ubera*, here, under the species
of worked lime-rock, that gave suck to the lord? She that
they already venerate (what other could they?)
her we declare?
Who else?[1]
And see how they run, the juxtaposed forms,
brighting the vaults of Lascaux; how the linear is wedded
to volume, how they do, within, in an unbloody manner,
under the forms of brown haematite and black manganese on
the graved lime-face, what is done, without,
far on the windy tundra
at the kill
that the kindred may have life.
O God!
O the Academies!

What ages since
his other marvel-day
when times turned?

---

[1] The reference is to the first work of plastic art in-the-round known to us,
the little limestone sculpture just over four inches high, of very ample proportions, known as 'the Venus of Willendorf'. It is dated, I believe, as contemporary with some of the recently discovered Lascaux cave-paintings, and is of
the same Aurignacian culture of 20-25,000 BC. If it is a 'Venus' it is very much a
Venus Genetrix, for it emphasizes in a very emphatic manner the nutritive and
generative physiognomy. It is rather the earliest example of a long sequence of
mother-figures, earth-mothers and mother goddesses, that fuse in the Great-
Mother of settled civilizations—not yet, by a long, long way, the Queen of
Heaven, yet, nevertheless, with some of her attributes; in that it images the
generative and the fruitful and the sustaining, at however primitive and elementary, or, if you will, 'animal' a level; though it is slovenly to use the word
'animal' of any art-form, for the making of such forms belongs only to man.

and *how* turned!
When
      (How?
      from early knocking stick or stane?)
the first New Fire wormed
      at the Easter of Technics.
What a holy Saturn's day!
O vere beata nox! [1]

                  A hundred thousand equinoxes
(less or more)
since they cupped the ritual stones
for the faithful departed. [2]

                        What, from this one's cranial data, is
like to have been his kindred's psyche; in that they, along
with the journey-food, donated the votive horn? and with
what *pietas* did they donate these among the dead—the life-
givers—and by what rubric?
Was their oral gloss from a Heidelberg gaffer or did they
emend a Piltdown use, was the girl from Lime Street a butty
of theirs, or were the eight Carmel fathers consanguine or of

---

[1] *O vere beata nox*, 'O truly blessed night'. See the *Exsultet* chanted by the
deacon at the blessing of the Paschal Candle which is lighted from a fire of
charcoal newly kindled by striking flint. This occurs once in the annual cycle,
in the spring, on Easter Saturday. From the new fire so kindled the lamps and
candles used during the ensuing twelve months are subsequently lit.

[2] Although Neanderthal man of 40 to 60,000 BC appears not to be regarded
by the anthropologists as a direct ancestor of ourselves, nevertheless it would
seem to me that he must have been 'man', for his burial-sites show a religious
care for the dead. At his places of interment the covering stones have revealed
ritual markings; moreover food-offerings, weapons and possibly a life-symbol
(a horn) have been found buried with him. Further, the hollow markings ('cup-
marks') are similar to those which characterize the sacred stones of tens of
thousands of years afterwards, in the New Stone Age culture which began, as
far as Western Europe is concerned, as recently as *c.* 5,000 BC, or later, to
continue among some primitive peoples to this day, in some parts of the world.

any affinity to those that fathered them, that told what they
had heard with their ears of those german to them, before the
palmy arbours began again to pine—and at which of the
boreal oscillations?

               And before them?
those who put on their coats to oblate the things set apart
in an older Great Cold.

               And who learned them
if not those whose fathers had received or aped the groping
disciplina of their cognates, or lost or found co-laterals, on
the proto-routes or at the lithic foci?

               Tundra-wanderers?
or was there no tundra as yet, or not as yet again, to wander
—but grew green the rashes over again? Or was all once again
informis, that Cronos for the third time might see how his
lemmings run and hear the cry of his tailless hare from south
of the sixties, from into the forties?

               For the phases and phase-groups
sway toward and fro within that belt of latitude.
There's where the world's a stage

               for transformed scenes
with metamorphosed properties

               for each shifted set.
Now naked as an imagined *belle sauvage*, or as is the actual
Mirriam.[1]

Now shirted, kilted, cloaked, capped and shod, as were the
five men of Jutland, discovered in their peaty cerements, or
as the bear-coped Gilyak is, or was, the other day.

---

[1] The Mirriam are a people of the Shendam Division of the Plateau Province
of Nigeria. The men of this tribe are not totally naked, but the women in
general are, except for ornaments of bamboo pith. I am indebted for this
information to Capt A. L. Milroy, MC, for many years a British official in that
area.

[62]

The mimes deploy:
>anthropoid
>anthropoi.

Who knows at what precise phase, or from what floriate green-room, the Master of Harlequinade, himself not made, maker of sequence and permutation in all things made, called us from our co-laterals out, to dance the Funeral Games of the Great Mammalia, as, long, long, long before, these danced out the Dinosaur?

Now, from the the draughty flats
>>the ageless cherubs

pout the Southerlies.

Now, Januarius brings in the millennial snow that makes the antlered mummers glow for many a hemera.

>The *Vorzeit*-masque is on

that moves to the cosmic introit.

Col canto the piping for this turn.

Unmeasured, irregular in stress and interval, of interior rhythm, modal.

>If tonic and final are fire

the dominant is ice
>>if fifth the fire

the cadence ice.

At these Nocturns the hebdomadary is apt to be vested for five hundred thousand weeks.[1]

Intunes the Dog:
>*Benedicite ignis* . . .

Cantor Notus and Favonius with all their south-aisled numina:

---

[1] Cf. the term Hebdomadarius, which is used of that member of a chapter or religious community whose office it is to lead in choir. His or her duties last a week.

> *con flora cálida*
> *mit warmer Fauna*

The Respond is with the Bear:

> *Benedicite frigus . . .*

Super-pellissed, stalled in crystallos, from the gospel-side, choir all the boreal schola

> *mit kalter Flora*
> *con fauna fría*

Now, sewn fibre is superfluous where Thames falls into Rhine. Now they would be trappers of every tined creature and make corners in ulotrichous hide and establish their wool-cartels as south as Los Millares. Where the stones shall speak of his cupola-makers:[1] but here we speak of long, long before their time.

> When is Tellus
> to give her dear fosterling
> her adaptable, rational, elect
> and plucked-out otherling
> a reasonable chance?
> Not yet—but soon, very soon
> as lithic phases go.

So before then?
> Did the fathers of those
> who forefathered them
> (if by genital or ideate begetting)
> set apart, make other, oblate?

By what rote, if at all
> had they the suffrage:
> Ascribe to, ratify, approve

---

[1] The first cupolas or rounded vaults in Europe were made by men of the Megalithic culture in Southern Spain, in the first and second millennium BC. We are, in our text, referring to conditions in the twentieth millennium BC or earlier.

in the humid paradises
      of the Third Age?[1]
But who or what, before these?
      Had they so far to reach the ground?
and what of the pelvic inclination of their co-laterals, whose
far cognates went—on how many feet?—in the old time
before *them*?
For all WHOSE WORKS FOLLOW THEM[2]
      among any of these or them
dona eis requiem.
      (He would lose, not any one
                 from among them.
Of all those given him
      he would lose none.)

      By the uteral marks
that make the covering stone an artefact.
      By the penile ivory
and by the viatic meats.
         Dona ei requiem.

---

[1] 'It was no doubt in the . . . Tertiary Age . . . that the earliest forms of man first came into existence' . . . 'Thus it was probably only after the expulsion of man from the Paradise of the Tertiary World . . . that he made those great primitive discoveries of the use of clothing, of weapons and above all of fire, which rendered him independent of the changes of climate. . . .' Dawson, *Age of the Gods*, 1929.

[2] See '. . . *opera enim illorum sequuntur illos*' in the Epistle for the Third Mass of All Souls' Day. *Apocalypse* xiv, 13. These *opera* are of course those that follow supernatural faith whereby the doers gain supernatural benefit. But I suppose it is permitted to use the same words analogously of those *opera* which we call artefacts, which man alone can cause to be.

The dictionary defines artefact as an artificial product, thus including the beaver's dam and the wren's nest. But I here confine my use of the word to those artefacts in which there is an element of the extra-utile and the gratuitous. If there is any evidence of this kind of artefacture then the artefacturer or artifex should be regarded as participating *directly* in the benefits of the Passion, because the extra-utile is *the* mark of man.

For which reason the description 'utility goods' if taken literally could refer only to the products of sub-man.

Who was he? Who?
Himself at the cave-mouth

                   the last of the father-figures
to take the diriment stroke

                  of the last gigantic leader of
thick-felled cave-fauna?
Whoever he was

                Dona ei requiem

sempiternam.
(He would not lose him

                 . . . *non perdidi*

ex eis quemquam.)[1]

                  Before the melt-waters
had drumlin-dammed a high hill-water for the water-maid
to lave her maiden hair.

Before they morained Tal-y-llyn, cirqued a high hollow for
Idwal, brimmed a deep-dark basin for Peris the Hinge and for
old Paternus.[2]

Long ages since they'd troughed, in solid Ordovician
his Bala bed for Tacitus.

---

[1] Quoted from the Good Friday Liturgy. '. . . I have not lost of them any
single one.'

[2] 'In places the irregularly eroded valley floors have been hollowed into true
rock basins and are now occupied by lakes, though most of the lakes are at least
in part dammed by morainic material.' *Brit. Reg. Geol. N. Wales*, p. 81. The
lake of Idwal, well above the 1,200 contour, six miles N.W. of Capel Curig,
occupies one such basin. The saint after whom Llanberis and Lake Peris are
named has, for some reason, acquired the description 'cardinal of Rome'. A
Peris son of Helig occurs in one genealogy.

Llyn Padarn means the Lake of Paternus: after Paternus 'of the red tunic',
grandfather of Cunedda, or after Padarn, the sixth-century saint? I suppose the
latter.

Long, long ago they'd turned the flow about.
But had they as yet morained
                    where holy Deva's entry is?
Or pebbled his mere, where
                    still the Parthenos
she makes her devious exit?[1]

Before the Irish sea-borne sheet lay tattered on the gestatorial
couch of Camber the eponym
                    lifted to every extremity of the sky
by pre-Cambrian oreos-heavers
                    for him to dream
the Combroges' epode.[2]
In his high *sêt*[3] there.
                    Higher than any of 'em
south of the Antonine limits.[4]
Above the sealed hypogéum
                    where the contest was
over the great *mundus* of sepulture (there the *ver-tigérnus* was)

---

[1] Bala Lake or Pimblemere is called in Welsh Llyn Tegid, the Lake of Tacitus. It may be noted that Tacitus was the name of Cunedda's great-grandfather. The basin is formed of solid rock but the S.W. end at least is thought to have been influenced by morainic deposits. At some remote geological period the outflow was southward, whereas now the Dee flows northward through the lake, but, says immemorial tradition, the two waters never mingle. Bala 'rhymes' with valour not with parlour.

[2] The word Cymry, kum-ry, the Welsh people, derives from the old Celtic compound *combrox* 'a person of the same kind', plural Combroges; pronounce kum-bro-gees, g hard, accent on middle syllable.

[3] *sêt* (Welsh ê *somewhat* resembles the a in 'cake'), seat, pew.

[4] The earth wall built between Clyde and Forth by Quinctius Lollius Urbicus in the reign of Antoninus Pius represented for a short while the outer *limes* of the empire in Britain.

here lie dragons and old Pendragons
>   very bleached. [1]
His uncomforming bed, as yet
>   is by the muses kept.

And shall be, so these Welshmen say, [2] till the thick rotundi-
ties give, and the bent flanks of space itself give way
>   and the whitest of the Wanderers
falters in her transit
>   at the Sibyl's *in favilla*-day. [3]

Before the drift
>   was over the lime-face.
Sometime between the final and the penultimate débâcle.
>   (Already Arcturus deploys his reconnoitering
chills in greater strength: soon his last *Putsch* on any scale.)
Before this all but proto-historic transmogrification of the
land-face.
Just before they rigged the half-lit stage for dim-eyed Clio
to step with some small confidence the measures of her
brief and lachrymal pavan.

---

[1] The Welsh name for the peak of Snowdon is Moel yr Wyddfa, the Hill of
the Burial Mound. Traditions of imprisoned dragons and buried heroes attach
to the site; *ver-tigérnus*, a 'chief lord'. Cf. Vortigern.

[2] When a Welsh poet of the eighteenth-century wished to express the final
catastrophe he wrote 'Snowdon's peak is one with the plain', just as Isaias or
John, had they been gentiles, would have written 'Olympus is brought low',
or 'Ida is cast into the sea'.

An analogous sentiment is to be detected in the twelfth-century Welshman
who told King Henry I that whatever policy he pursued, Welshness would
endure until the dissolution of all things.

[3] See the hymn by Thomas of Celano, *Dies Irae*.
'day on which the world dissolves into ashes (*in favilla*) as David and the
Sibyl testify.'

Before, albescent, out of the day-starred neoarctic night the
Cis-Alclyde¹ pack again came sud of the Mull.

                       Across the watersphere
over the atmosphere, preventing the crystal formations
ambient grew the wondrous New Cold:

                       trauma and thauma, both.
This is how Cronos reads the rubric, *frangit per medium*, when
he breaks his ice like morsels, for the therapy and fertility
of the land-masses.²
Or before

           from Eden-dales, or torn from the becked fells
                  transmontane
                  transmarine
the barrier-making flood-gravels
the drumlined clays and the till-drift

               had bye-wayed and delta'd the mainway
for Tanat and Vyrnwy.

             Before the heaped detritus
had parted the nymphaean loves

               of naiad Sabrina and sibylline Dee.³

---

¹ Cis-Alclyde. The old name for the Rock of Dumbarton was Altclut, or
Petra Cloithe, the Rock in the Clyde. It was from just south of the Clyde, from
the Southern Uplands of Scotland, that the deposits were carried into the Mid-
land Plain of England and into the Plain of Gwent and elsewhere in Wales. See
note 1 to page 73 below.

² See the rubric directing the celebrant at the point of the Mass called the
Fraction. 'He . . . takes the host and breaks it in half (*frangit per medium*) over
the chalice.'

Cf. also Psalm CXLVII, 17, Bk of Com. Pr version. 'He casteth forth his
ice like morsels: who is able to abide his frost?'

³ The courses of the rivers Tanat, Vyrnwy, Severn and Dee have all been
affected by glacial action. The latter two flowed as one, but the Severn was later
caused to flow east and mingle with the Stour while the Dee took its present
course north through the border lands gathering to itself many associations
and coming to be regarded as a sacred stream. Indeed some have interpreted
its Welsh name, Dyfrdwy, as meaning the 'divine water'.

She must marl her clear cascade-locks in dawdling Stour's
English bed

                                   and she
must glen her parthenogenic waters a shorter cut by Gwenfrewi's well, before she comes to Wirral. ¹
Before, trans-Solway

                and from over Manannan's *moroedd*, the last debris-
freighted floes echeloned solid from Monapia to Ynys Fôn²

                discharged on Arfon *colles*
what was cargoed-up on Grampius Mons.

                Off the 'strath' into the *ystrad*
out of the 'carse' on to the *traeth*. ³
Heaped amorphous

                out of Caledonia
into Cambria⁴

                bound for Snowdonia
transits Cumbria.

                Long, long, long before
(fifty thousands of winter calends?

---

¹ Gwenfrewi, in English, Winefred, whose sacred well gave the English
name Holywell and the Welsh name Treffynnon (homestead+spring) to that
site a mile-and-a-half only from where the estuary of the Dee divides the two
nations.

² Manannan mac Lir, in Welsh Manawydan mab Llyr, the sea god; *moroedd*,
seas, mor-roithe. Monapia, the name of the Isle of Man in Pliny. Ynys Fôn,
un-iss von, o as in vote, the Island of Mona, Anglesey.

³ The elements 'strath' and 'carse' in Scottish place-names have a correspondence with *ystrad*, us-trad (vale, flats) and *traeth*, ae as ah+eh (shore,
estuary) in Welsh ones.

⁴ Caledonia is sometimes made to mean the Highlands, but here I use it as
a synonym for Scotland and in particular for the Southern Uplands, because it
was from this southern area that geological deposits of the Ice Age and certain
legendary and historical deposits of the sub-Roman age came to Wales.
For instance, in spite of medieval pseudo-history, 'King Cole' has no relationship with Colchester, but is the *Coil hen guotepauc* of Harleian MS. 3859 and is
to be associated with the district of Kyle in Ayrshire. In 1912 in Camberwell a
Miss Williams said to me, 'On my father's side I am descended from Coel
Hên Godebog'. It is the boast of many old Welsh families.

fifty thousand calends of Maia before?)

>   the Lord Cunedda[1]

conditor noster

>   *filius Æterni*, son of Padarn Red
Pexa,[2] son of Tacitus, came south over the same terrain and
by way of the terrain-gaps then modified or determined: for
the *viae* are not independent of geology: that his hobnailed[3]
foederati, his twelve cantred-naming sons[4] and himself, the
loricated leader in his gaffer's purple, might scrape from their
issue *caligae* the mud of Forth into Conwy.

Clyde into Clwyd.

>   Otadini

over Venedotia

>   and even in Irish Demetia

a Cunedda's Hill.

>   Combroges bore us:

---

[1] Cunedda, kin-eth-ah, th as in nether, accent on middle syllable.

[2] The grandfather of Cunedda is known in the Welsh genealogies as Padarn
Beisrudd. *Beis* is a mutation of *peis*, a coat, petticoat or tunic, and is known to
derive direct from the Latin *pexus, pexa*, descriptive of a woollen fabric that
had not lost its nap, thence something new and well cared for, and as a metonym
it came to be used of the garment called the *tunica*.

The Welsh word *rudd* meant crimson red.

These considerations tend to support the view, now held by historians, that
the family of Cunedda had a tradition of holding office under the Roman imperium. 'Beisrudd' might possibly imply the *tunica* with the broad purple
laticlave, associated with rank, or the all-purple *tunica* associated with military
command, or with some other dyed garment of legatine significance.

[3] The absence of archaeological evidence from the burial-places of sub-
Roman Britain contrasts with the considerable evidence from the graves of the
Saxon invaders. There is, however, one thing which archaeology has shown: a
number of Britons of this period who died, or were buried, with their boots
on, had hob-nails in their boots. We know also that the field-service boot
(*caliga*) of the Roman army was similarly studded.

[4] The *Historia Brittonum* gives the number of Cunedda's sons as twelve, other
evidence supposes nine. Six of these gave their names to Welsh cantreds or to
lesser divisions of land.

tottering, experienced, crux-signed

                     old Roma

the yet efficient mid-wife of us. [1]

              Before the slow estuarine alchemies had coal-
blacked the green dryad-ways over the fire-clayed seat-earth
along all the utile seams from Taff to Tâf. [2]

Before the microgranites and the clay-bonded erratics
wrenched from the diorites of Aldasa, or off the Goat Height
in the firth-way, or from the Clota-sides or torn from either
Dalriada, [3] with what was harrowed-out *in via*, up, from the

---

[1] It is generally accepted that the man known to Welsh tradition as Cunedda
Wledig was a Romanized Briton, almost certainly a Christian, and possibly
associated with the office of Dux Britanniarum. Sometime before the year
AD 400, he came, presumably under Roman auspices, from the district of the
Otadini or Votadini in South Scotland, into Venedotia (N. Wales). His great-
grandfather, his grandfather, his father and three of his nine(?) sons and one of
his grandsons bore Roman names; two of which, Donatus and Marianus, are
said to be certainly of Christian provenance. The rule which these men established in Wales, in the age of St Ambrose, was destined to evolve into a
dynasty of native princes, which endured, in however precarious a fashion, for
nine centuries.

    Demetia (S.W. Wales) was held by Irish settlers. Nennius (AD 800) says
that Cunedda cleared this area also, but this is denied by modern historians.
Nevertheless there is, near Kidwelly, a hill called Allt Cunedda.

    [2] Symbolically speaking only, these two rivers can be said to bound, on the
east and on the west, the South Wales coalfield. Taff rhymes with saff in saffron,
but Tâf (tahv) rhymes with calve.

    [3] Pronounce dal-ree-adda, accent on ad. I follow the present Scottish pronun-
ciation as told to me by a native of Dumbarton.

    There was a kingdom of Dalriada on the Irish side also; indeed it was the
invasions of the Dalriad Scots from Ireland that gave the names Scotland and
Dalriada to parts of northern Britannia.

long drowned out-crops, under, coalesced and southed by
the North Channel. [1]

      As though the sea itself were sea-borne
and under weigh
         as if the whole Ivernian *mare*
directed from hyperboreal control-points by strategi of the
axis were one complex of formations in depth, moving on a
frontage widening with each lesser degree of latitude.

          Heading toward, right astride
to one degree beyond
        Ffraid Santes' [2] fire-track
where Brendan shall cry from his sea-horse
Mirabilis Deus in sanctis suis! [3]

From before all time
        the New Light beams for them
and with eternal clarities
        infulsit and athwart
the fore-times:

---

[1] 'Contemporaneous with the glaciers of North Wales, ice sheets from the
Clyde Valley and the Southern Uplands of Scotland, from the Lake District and
from the heights of north-eastern Ireland descended and converged into the
depression of the Irish Sea. From this area of congestion the combined flows
moved southward under great pressure, part escaping directly by way of St
George's Channel, but part thrust against the land mass of North Wales.'
Bernard Smith and T. Neville George in *Brit. Reg. Geol. N. Wales*, pp. 77-8.

[2] Ffraid Santes, St Bride, Brigit. *Ffraid* rhymes approx. with bride and
Santes approx. with aunt. + ess. Cf. the association of Brigit with fire-rites;
and cf. St Bride's Bay, Pembs, an area of water covered by the ice-sheets.

[3] The glaciation reached to about 51 deg. North Lat., thus extending just
beyond the waters between South Wales and Ireland, which very many millennia
later were to become associated with the marvel-voyages of the Celtic ascetics;
such as the navigation-saint, Brendan, who in the legend rides the narrow
channel on a marine creature and hails Finbar, mounted on David's swimming
horse, with the words 'God is marvellous in his saints'.

[73]

era, period, epoch, hemera.
Through all orogeny:
group, system, series, zone.
Brighting at the five life-layers
species, species, genera, families, order.
Piercing the eskered silt, discovering every stria, each score
and macula, lighting all the fragile laminae of the shales.
However Calypso has shuffled the marked pack, veiling with
early the late.
Through all unconformities and the sills without sequence,
glorying all the under-dapple.
Lighting the Cretaceous and the Trias, for Tyrannosaurus
must somehow lie down with herbivores, or, the poet lied,
which is not allowed.
However violent the contortion or whatever the inversion
of the folding.
Oblique through the fire-wrought cold rock dyked from
convulsions under.
Through the slow sedimentations laid by his patient creature
of water.
Which ever the direction of the strike, whether the hade is
to the up-throw or the fault normal.
Through all metamorphs or whatever the pseudomorphoses.

As, down among the palaeo-zoe
he brights his ichthyic sign
so brights he the middle-zone
where the uterine forms
are some beginnings of his creature.
Brighter yet over the mammal'd Pliocene
for these continuings
certainly must praise him:
How else, in his good time
should the amorous Silvy

                    to her sweetest dear
her fairest bosom have shown?[1]

                    How else we?
                    or he, himself?
whose name is called He-with-us
because he did not abhor the uterus.
                    Whereby these uberal forms
are to us most dear
                    and of all hills
the most august.

How else her iconography?
How other his liturgy?
                    Masters and doctors
of seven-breasted Roma
or of all sites that offer nurture
                    of which it is said
Hinc lucem et pocula sacra[2]
                    or you of Rhydychen[3]
that have the Lord for your light:
                    Answer me!

---

[1] Cf. *On a Time the Amorous Silvy*, verse 2.
                    'With that her fairest bosom showing,
                    Op'ning her lips, rich perfumes blowing,
                    She said, Now kiss me and be going,
                    My sweetest dear!'
    John Attey. *The First Booke of Ayres Of Four Parts, With Tableture for the Lute*,
1622.

[2] 'From this place light and a sacred potion.'

[3] Pronounce rhid-uch-en, accent on middle syllable; from *rhyd*, ford, and
ychen, oxen; *ch* as in Scottish *loch*.

¹ For the uncovering of the bones of the earliest known South Wallian at the oldest burial-site in Britain we are indebted to the Rev William Buckland, Reader in Geology in the University of Oxford, who made his discovery in 1822, and called it the Red Lady. These remains were in association with those of mammoth and elk and other fauna of Palaeolithic times. It is now established that the skeleton was that of a man about twenty-five years old. He had been buried with rites, in a cerement of powdered red oxide of iron, signifying life; with rods of ivory and wearing ornaments of the same 'incorruptible' substance. When this man's body was committed to the Paviland lime-rock in Gower ten miles or so south-west of Swansea, we can presume that some of his continental contemporaries were engaged upon such works as those which the little French boys and their dog stumbled upon in the Lascaux caves in 1940. Works which have since proved a reassurance to us all, that man, already, 20 to 40,000 years ago, whatever his limitations or capabilities was capable of superb artistry. In some respects we have not again equalled that artistry, let alone surpassed it.

² Mr Jackson Knight writes: 'Proserpina, queen of the dead, was thought to mark for death all who died, by cutting a lock of their hair as hair is cut from animals to mark them for sacrifice'. Proserpine, that brings with her the spring, stands for death in general, so then for that particular death, indeed particularly for that death which is 'shown forth' and 'recalled' in the eucharist. Further, in the rite of the fourth-century Egyptian bishop, Serapion, the eucharist is regarded as a recalling of all the dead: 'We entreat also on behalf of all who have fallen asleep, of which this (i.e. this action) is the recalling'. Here 'all who have fallen asleep' refers to the departed members of the Christian community in Egypt and throughout the world, because no institution can, in its public formulas, presume the membership of any except those who have professed such membership. But over and above these few there are those many, of all times and places, whose lives and deaths have been made acceptable by the same Death on the Hill of which every Christian breaking of bread is an epiphany and a recalling.

With regard to the Upper Palaeolithic South Welshman buried in Paviland, it would seem that Theology allows us to regard him among the blessed by forbidding us to assert the contrary.

³ This particular variant of the sheep-score is used here because it happens to be the only one I know. It is from Lancashire. As with all the variants from different parts of England it is a corruption of the ordinary Welsh cardinal numbers. It is sometimes questioned whether these immemorial English uses have come down direct from the Celtic-speaking population of previous to the Anglo-Saxon invasions, or whether they derive from later contacts with the Welsh sheep-trade. For many reasons the latter seems extremely unlikely. Moreover, the association of sheep with Wales is relatively modern, being in part due to Cistercian enterprise in the thirteenth century, and as late as Queen Anne the typical Welsh stock was cattle rather than sheep.

MINERVA·IOVIS

QVIA·PER·IN
CARNATI· ✳
VERBI·MYS
TERIVM·N
OVA·MEN
TIS·NOST
RÆ·OCVLIS·
LVX·TVÆ·
CLARITATIS·
INFVLSIT

CAPITE·ORTA

                              Brighting totally
the post-Pliocene
both Pleistocene and Recent.

                              An aureole here
for Europa's tundra-*beata*
who of duck's bone had made her needle-case.
And where the carboniferous floor
yields from among the elk-bones and the breccia
this separated one
            the data of whose cause is known alone to *him*.

The *egregius*

                              young, toward the prime,
wearing the amulets of ivory and signed with the life-giving
ochre. [1]

                  Strayed from among the nine and ninety
Aurignacian *beati*
                  that he has numbered
at his secret shearing
                  as things made over
                  by his Proserpine
                              to himself. [2]
When on a leafy morning
            late in June
against the white wattles
            he numbers his own.

As do they
            taught of the herdsman's *Ordinale*
and following the immemorial *numeri*
who say:
            Yan, tyan, tethera, methera, pimp
sethera, lethera, hovera, dovera, dick. [3]

For whom he has notched
his crutched tally-stick
              not at: less one five twenties
              but
at *centum*[1]
       that follow the Lamb
from the Quaternary dawn.
       Numbered among his flock
that no man may number
       but whose works follow them.

Searching where the kitchen midden tells of the decline
which with the receding cold marked the recession of the
Magdalenian splendours.
Yet there he brights fragmented protomorphs
where lies the rudimentary bowl.[2]

                                                    How else

multifariam multisque modis[3]
              the splendour of forms yet to come?

---

[1] Various local traditions prevail as to the marking of the tally. In parts of
Wales a notch is made in the stick for every ten sheep counted and in parts of
the Lake District the hand is raised for every twenty and the tally notched for
every hundred.

One Welsh way of saying 'ninety-nine' is 'except one, five twenties' (*amyn
un pum ugain*). This is used in the Welsh gospel where St Luke reports our
Lord as saying, in terms of the hill-people from whom he came: 'What man of
you, having an hundred sheep, if he lose one, etc.' He was addressing Aramaean
canonists, but he spoke as though to Powell Chapel Farm, Lewis the Vision or
Watkins Tal Sarn.

[2] Rather oddly, the first beginnings of anything like pottery are found among
the depressed peoples who lived after the decline of the Palaeolithic cultures
and before the rise of the Neolithic.

[3] See the Epistle for the Third Mass of Christmas Day, Heb. I, 1. '. . . at
sundry times and in divers manners'.

How the dish
>> that holds no coward's food?[1]

How the *calix*
>> without which
>> how *the* re-calling?

And there
>> where, among the exactly faceted microliths[2]
>> lie the bones
of the guardian and friend.
>> How else Argos
the friend of Odysseus?
>> Or who should tend
the sores of lazars?
(For anthropos is not always kind.)
>> How Ranter or True, Ringwood
>> or the pseudo-Gelert?[3]
>> How Spot, how Cerberus?
(For men can but proceed from what they know, nor is it for
the mind of this flesh to practise poiesis, *ex nihilo*.)
How the hound-bitches
>> of the stone kennels of Arthur
that quested the hog and the brood of the hog

---

[1] In Welsh mythology, when Arthur goes to raid the Celtic hades one of the spoils he has to recover is a vessel from which no coward can eat or drink.

[2] To the same Mesolithic epoch of the first beginnings of pottery belongs also the first domestication of the dog. This was during a low ebb of prehistoric culture, yet the pygmy weapon-heads are famous: 'their microliths, although often measuring no more than half an inch long, are yet meticulously trimmed' write J. and C. Hawkes in *Prehistoric Britain*.

[3] I use the mutated form, Gelert, because this is familiar and customary; the radical form is Celert and is the name of a man, presumably a sixth-century saint. The hound-association at Beddgelert is said to be not older than the Romantic Revival of the eighteenth-nineteenth centuries. There are, however, tales of devoted Welsh hounds of early date (Cf. Giraldus) from which the Gelert *motif* may stem.

from Pebidiog to Aber Gwy?
How the dog Toby? How the flew'd sweet thunder for
dewy Ida?[1]

And over the submerged dryad-ways
intensively his ray searches

                where the alluvium holds
the polished neoliths
and where the long mound inhumes

                his neolithic loves
or the round-barrow keeps

                the calcined bones
of these, his still more modern hallows

                that handled the pitiless bronze.

(Pray for her by whom came war

                for whose urn-burial
  they made the cist four-square

                on the bank of the Alaw.)[2]

---

[1] Cf. the names of certain of the megaliths of South Wales: 'The Stone of the Greyhound Bitch', 'The Kennel of the Greyhound Bitch', 'The Stone of the Children of Arthur', 'The Enclosure of Arthur', etc.

If the hunt of the boar Trwyth by the men and dogs of Arthur described in the tale of *Culhwch* is read with one eye on the Ordnance Survey's map, the Distribution of the Megaliths (sheet 7), the possibility of some connection between the itinerary of this great mythological hunt and the sites of the megaliths may suggest itself. Pebidiog is the south-west extremity of Wales where the hog and his pigs came in from Ireland. Aber Gwy (gooy) means Mouth of the Wye, where the hog escaped into the Severn estuary, to be overtaken in Cornwall and to be driven into the Atlantic. Cf. also *Mids. N.D.* IV, 1.

[2] Cf. the *mabinogi* of Branwen daughter of Llyr in *The Mabinogion*, Gwyn and Thomas Jones trans. *Everyman* edtn 1949.

'Alas, son of God, said she, . . . two good islands have been laid waste because of me . . . and with that her heart broke. And a four-sided grave was made for her and she was buried there on the bank of the Alaw.'

In 1813 an Anglesey farmer requiring stone for repairs is said to have uncovered a mound by the River Alaw and to have found a square cist containing a funerary urn. This is said to have occurred on a site traditionally known as 'Bronwen's Island'. Alaw rhymes with vow, accent on 'Al'.

And over the Cis-padane marls
searching the trapezoidal platforms:
   for but for the Terramare *disciplina*
how should his Mantuan have sung
     the Quadrilateral Plan?[1]

Upon all fore-times.
     From before time
his perpetual light
     shines upon them.
     Upon all at once
upon each one
whom he invites, bids, us to recall
when we make the recalling of him
      daily, at the Stone.
When the offerant
   our *servos*, so theirs whose life is changed
not taken away[2]
     is directed to say
      Memento etiam.
After which it is allowed him then to say
      Nobis quoque.
That we too may be permitted some part with these
like John is!

---

[1] Cf. the opinion of scholars that the rectilineal layout of camps and cities characteristic of Rome and the Latin civilization was derived from the Bronze Age agriculturalists of the Po Valley who constructed their solid pile settlements with great care for alignment and consistent orientation, with intersecting streets, the whole forming a trapezoid. See page 55 above.

[2] See the preface in the Mass for All Souls' Day and for all Masses of the departed '. . . Tuis enim fidelibus, Domine, vita mutatur non tollitur'. 'For thy faithful, O Lord, life is changed not taken away.'

as is Felicity.¹
Through the same Lord
that gave the naiad her habitat
which is his proto-sign.
How else from the weathered mantle-rock
and the dark humus spread
(where is exacted the night-labour
where the essential and labouring worm
saps micro-workings all the dark day long²
for his creature of air)
should his barlies grow
who said
I am your Bread?

*   *   *

¹ The commemoration of the dead in the Latin rite follows the consecration
and begins: 'Remember them, O Lord, thy servants'. This prayer for the departed is followed immediately by: 'To us also, sinners, grant some part . . .
with John, etc., Felicity, etc., . . . into whose company admit us . . . through
Christ our Lord'. The prayer concludes with a kind of recalling of the fruits
of the land ('hallow, quicken and bless these and give them to us') without
which no sacrament could be.

² Darwin, in *The Formation of Vegetable Mould through the Action of Worms*,
Ch. I, says in effect that worms do their 'day-labour light deny'd' in two senses,
in that they work only by night and are blind, yet are far from being insensitive
to light.

General Note to Section I. The findings of the physical sciences are necessarily
mutable and change with fresh evidence or with fresh interpretation of the same
evidence. This is an important point to remember with regard to the whole of
this section of my text where I employ ideas based on more or less current interpretations of archaeological and anthropological data. Such interpretations, of
whatever degree of probability, remain hypothetical. The layman can but employ for his own purposes the pattern available during his lifetime. The poet in
c. 1200 could make good use of a current supposition that a hill in Palestine
was the centre of the world. The poet of the seventeenth-century could make
use of the notion of gravitational pull. The abiding truth behind those two
notions would now, in both cases (I am told), be differently expressed. But the
poet, of whatever century, is concerned only with how he can use a current
notion to express a permanent mythus.

II

MIDDLE-SEA AND LEAR-SEA

Twelve hundred years
                    close on
since of the Seven grouped Shiners
                    one doused her light. 1
Since Troy fired
                    since they dragged him
                    widdershins 2
without the wall.
When they regarded him:
his beauties made squalid, his combed gilt
                    a matted mop
his bruised feet thonged
                    under his own wall.
Why did they regard him
the decorous leader, *neque decor* . . . 3
volneraque illa gerens 4 . . . many of them
under his dear walls? 5

---

1 At the fall of Troy one of the Pleiades is said to have been extinguished.

2 It is to be supposed that Achilles, in chasing, or in the other tradition, dragging, Hector around the defences of Troy, did so anti-sunwise; as it was to unbind the protection of the city and not to secure it. (See on this matter, Jackson Knight *Virgil's Troy*, p. 23, and *Cumaean Gates*, p. 90.)

3 See Isaias LIII, 2, '*non est species et neque decor*', (Vulgate) 'there is no beauty in him nor comeliness'. (A.V.)

4 See 'Squalentem barbam et concretos sanguine crines
        Volneraque illa gerens quae circum plurima muros
        Accipit patrios.' *Aeneid II* 277-9.

5 See what is said above of Hector, 'His beard made squalid, his hair concreted with blood, bearing the many wounds he had received around the wall of his *patria*', and also 'O light of the whole Trojan world' and '*Heu mihi!* what was his aspect now, and how changed' and 'By what intolerable cause are your bright features made horrible to us' and other such phrases referring to the defilement of the beauty of the hero in *Aeneid II*. All this inevitably recalls 'he had no beauty that we should desire him . . . yet did we esteem stricken', etc., and other passages in the Prophets and also in the narrative of the Passion itself and in subsequent devotional writings, concerning the indignities suffered by the Redeemer, both within and without the walls of his *patria*.

What centuries less
       since the formative epochs, the sign-years in Saturn's
tellus,[1] in the middle lands of it? For even for the men with
the *groma*,[2] even for the men of rule, whose *religio* is rule
                for the world-orderers
                for the world-syndicate
even for us
       whose robbery is conterminous with empire[3]
there was a: Once there was . . .
and wonder-years
and wanderers tall tale to tell
               anabasis
               by sea, by land
               fore-chosen site
          decalogue, dodecalogue graven
               tabernacled flame
               palladia come down.

Him up to heaven
               in chariot-fire.[4]
The heaven-appointed beast of grey
           to nourish the lily-white pair.
Horsed Dioscuri
              to make 'em shape
restoring at the smothered centre, adjuvant at the caving

---

[1] Saturn's *tellus*=Italy.

[2] The Roman surveyor's measuring instrument.

[3] Cf. Augustine, *City of God*, IV, 4.

[4] It will be recalled that the 'Twelve Tables' of Roman tradition were originally ten, that the temple of Vesta tabernacled the sacred fire, that the sacred
shields came down from, that Romulus was assumed up to, heaven; that Scrip-
tural tradition offers certain near parallels. We Europeans have participated of
both traditions—of the one by right of cultural and racial inheritance, of the
other by 'adoption and grace'—*Teste David cum Sibylla*.

flank; the watering of mounts last groomed at heaven's horse-
lines, the care of celestial arms, their working parts fouled
in terrestrial war, the scrubbing-off of front-area muck from
unearthly equipment at a pond, in the market-place

      in broad day
      as large as life
            a thing seen of many
    so they do say. [1]

             (They can show you the piscene.) [2]

      How long, since
on the couch of time
      departed myth
left ravished fact
till Clio, the ageing mid-wife, [3] found her
nine calends gone
      huge in labour with the Roman people?
[O, him! she said,
      himself, m'lord
the square-pushing Strider, [4] him?
and how should I?

---

[1] Cf. the traditions surrounding the battle of Lake Regillus which, very long
before we had so much as heard of Livy, the majority of us learned by heart from
The Lays and owing to the easy facility of Macaulay's rhymes are unable, if we
would, to forget. From Macaulay we first sensed that we belonged to the
Roman world and that Vesta, Juno, Romulus, Praeneste, 'reedy Thrasymene',
and most of all 'the Great Asylum', had an evocative power over us.

[2] I am told the fountain where Castor and Pollux washed their armour after
the Battle of Lake Regillus is still shown to visitors in Rome.

[3] *Kleio*, 'she that extols', the Muse of History.

[4] Perhaps it has already become necessary to note that around about the period
1914-18 and subsequently, a 'square-pusher' was a soldier out courting. I do
not know if the expression is still current among soldiers.
See the surname of Mars, *Gradivus*.

It was dark, a very stormy night—the projecting cheek-guards, the rigid nasal-piece—brazen he wore it and darked his visage; twin-crested, and his mantling horse-tail shadowed dark *murex* my fair Aryan shoulders. Not he—not his proofed thorax neither, nor had he gratitude to unlace the mired greaves of surly iron—the squat Georgie!

B'the clod smell on him *that's* what he *was*—before he got his papers[1], by the manners of him. Yet—Verticordia, prevent us continually! but *which* way should grace turn matriarch-hearts?[2] . . . and how his glory filled the whole place where we were together.

And, now that I recall it:

he first, with his butt-iron, marked the intersection and squared a space—he took his own time on that—and signed me to stand by, then, with a beck of his elbow, turned m' ample front to constant Arcturus, himself aligned to the southward, minding his dressing like the foot-mob masher he was,—or a haruspex checking his holy stance,

the terrible inaugurator!

and, at the intersected place he caused our sacred commerce to be. Why yes—west he took himself off, on the base-line he traced and named when he traced it: *decumanus*. West-turn from his *kardo* I saw him go, over his right *transversus*.[3] From to rear of him I discerned his marcher's lurch—I'd breath to see that.

West-star, hers and all!

brighting the hooped turn of his scapular-plates enough

---

[1] Mars was an agriculturalist before he was a soldier.

[2] Venus, under the title Verticordia, Turner of Hearts, was supplicated as the special guardian of fidelity and in this capacity was the patroness of matrons.

[3] Cf. the sacred routine followed by the Roman surveyors in the laying out of sites: the north-south bearing was called *kardo* and the east-west was called *decumanus,* and the left and right limits of the square were each called *limes transversus.*

to show his pelvic sway and the hunch on his robber's
shoulders. Though he was of the Clarissimi his aquila over
me was robbery. [1]
'T's a great robbery
                    —is empire.]

Half a millennium or so
                    since
                    out went the Lucomos
since we became
                    abasileutos.
A good year?
                    But little more
(the Kalends are erased or never reckoned)
since those hidden years
when an armaments commission
                    (Tuscan at that)
could and did
effectively proscribe us:
                    plant
                    operatives
                    raw metal.
That takes you back
                    and aback.
The Urbs without edged iron
                    can you credit it?
                    Nudge Clio
she's apt to be musing.
Slap her and make her extol
                    all or nothing.

---

[1] Cf. Song of Songs, II, 4, 'and his banner over me was love'. And cf. how
those training for the Survey used the title Clarissimus.

Five hundred and thirty-nine years since the first consular
year and the beginnings of the less uncertain sequences and
the more defined contours.
How long since first we began to contrive
                        on the loose-grained tufas
quarried about the place;
                        incise, spaced and clear
on the carried marbles
                        impose on the emblems:
S E N A T U S P O P U L U S Q U E . . . ?
                        for all the world-nurseries
to say: Roma knows great A.[1]
For the world-connoisseurs to cant their necks and to allow:
        Yes, great epigraphers, let's grant 'em one perfected
aesthetic—and, of course, there's the portrait-busts.

        One hundred and sixty-seven years
since Tiberius Gracchus
                    wept for the waste-land
and the end of the beginnings
                   . . . and where I had a vineyard
on a very fruitful hill fenced and watered
                    the syndicate's agent
pays-off the ranch operatives
                    (his bit from the Urbs
waits in the car).

---

[1] I had in mind a child's rhyme which I can but hazily recall, but which I
think ran somewhat as follows:
                'Tiddle taddle titmouse
                Flora* knows great A
                B and C and D and E
                G, H, I and J and K.'
  * Or Doris, or Augustus or whatever the name of the child reciting it.

But sixty-eight years, since
                    in came the Principate
and the beginnings of the end and the waxing of the megalo-
polis and the acute coarsening of the forms, the conscious
revivals, the eclectic grandeur
                    . . . the grand years
since we began our
                    Good Time Coming.
And already, on every commodity and on the souls of men,
the branded numerals: *sexcenti sexaginta sex*. [1]

One thousand two hundred years
                    since the Dorian jarls
rolled up the map of Arcady and the transmontane storm-
groups fractured the archaic pattern.
                    Within the hoop
of the iron years
                    the age is obscure—
and is the age dark?
          The makers of anathemata can, at a pinch, beat out
utile spares for the mobile columns or amulets for the raiding
captains and the captains themselves bring certain specifica-
tions and new god-fears.
The adaptations, the fusions
the transmogrifications
                    but always
the inward continuities
                              of the site
                              of place.

---

[1] Cf. The Apocalypse of St John, xiii, 16-18.

From the tomb of the strife-years the new-born shapes begin already to look uncommonly like the brats of mother Europa.
We begin already to discern our own.
Are the proto-forms already ours?
Is that the West-wind on our cheek-bones?

But it's early—very grey and early in our morning and most irradiance is yet reflected from far-side Our Sea, the Nile moon still shines on the Hittite creatures and Crete still shows the Argives how.

Six centuries
                and the second Spring
and a new wonder under heaven:
                man-limb stirs
                        in the god-stones
and the kouroi
                are gay and stepping it
but stanced solemn.
And now is given a new stone indeed:
                the Good Calf-herd
for Rhonbos his *pastor bonus*
lifted up and adored
(and may we say of his moschophoros:
this pastoral Lord *regit me?*)[1]

---

[1] Cf. the superb early sixth-century-BC fragmentary marble figure of a man carrying a calf dedicated by a person called Rhonbos on the Acropolis. One is inevitably reminded of the centuries later, immeasurably inferior, well-known Graeco-Roman figure called the 'Good Shepherd', adaptations of which are familiar to Christians. The smile on a kouros is Greek, the stance Egyptian.

Cf. also the opening words of the Vulgate Psalm 22, 'The Lord rules me', which is Ps 23 in the A.V., 'The Lord is my Shepherd'.

and the Delectable Korê:
by the radial flutes for her chiton, the lineal, chiselled hair
the contained rhythm of her
            is she Elenê Argive
or is she transalpine Eleanore
or our Gwenhwyfar[1]
            the Selenê of Thulê
            West-Helen?
She's all that and more
all korai, all parthenai made stone.[2]

Agelastos Petra . . .[3]
     and yet you smile from your stone.

          Not again, not now again
till on west-portals
in Gallia Lugdunensis
           when the Faustian lent[4] is come
and West-wood springs new
           (and Christ the thrust of it!)
and loud sings West-cuckoo
           (Polymnia, how shrill!)
     will you see her like
         if then.

---

[1] Gwenhwyfar, gwen-hooy-varr, stress accent on the middle syllable; Guenevere.

[2] I was thinking in particular of the sixth-century-BC Athenian statuette of a young woman, known to connoisseurs as the 'Beautiful Kore', and of others of the archaic period which in some ways share a certain similarity of feeling with some carved queens of the twelfth-century-AD in the West—at Chartres for instance. Kore, maiden; korai, parthenai, maidens.

[3] Agelastos Petra, 'the laughless rock'. See note 1 to page 56 above.

[4] The reference is to Spengler's use of the term 'Faustian' which he employs to describe the Celto-Latin-Germanic-Western-Christian culture which by his theory had its springtime in the earliest middle ages. This is to say its freshest vitality was over before 1300.

Not again
        till the *splendor formarum*[1]
        when, under West-light
                the Word is made stone.
And when
        where, how or ever again?
                        . . . or again?
Not ever again?
        never?
After the conflagrations
        in the times of forgetting?
in the loops between?
before the prides
        and after the happy falls?

Spes!
        answer me!!
How right you are—
        blindfold's best!
        But, where d'you think the flukes of y'r hook'll hold
next—from the *feel* of things?

Down we come
        quick, but far
to the splendours
        to the skill-years

---

[1] Cf. the technical term *splendor formae* used of Beauty in Thomist philosophy. I borrow the terminology to use it analogously and in a non-philosophical, everyday sense and in the plural, of those visible 'forms' of art-works, which, after all, derive their outward 'splendour' from the *forma*, i.e. the unseen in-forming principle, referred to in the technical language of the definition.

and the signed and fine grandeurs.
O yes, technique—but much more:
the god still is balanced
$\qquad$ in the man-stones
$\quad$ but it's a nice thing
as near a thing as ever you saw.

One hundred and seventeen olympiads
since he contrived her:
$\qquad$ chryselephantine
$\qquad$ of good counsel
$\qquad$ within
$\qquad\quad$ her Maiden's chamber
$\qquad$ tower of ivory
$\qquad\quad$ in the gilded *cella*
$\qquad$ herself a house of gold.
Her grandeurs
$\quad$ enough and to snare:
$\qquad$ West-academic
$\qquad$ West-hearts.
And her that he cast of Marathon-salvage
$\qquad$ of bronze
$\qquad$ erect
$\qquad$ without
$\qquad$ Promachos
$\qquad$ of the polis
$\qquad$ of Ouranos
Virgo Potens
$\quad$ her alerted armament
land-mark for sea-course
Polias, and star of it
$\quad$ but Tritogenian.
As a sea-mark then
$\quad$ for the navigating officers.

Not always: *blue* Aegean
                nor smiling middle-*mare*.
The loomings and the dippings
                unsighted
what jack she wore
                unrecognized.
Who are you pray?[1]
                unanswered.
(Low, raked, Pelasgian Long Serpent
                for the low sea-mist.)
The shifts of wind
                the intermittent rain
                    but Sunium
rounded.
Thirty-seven forty-five north
twenty-three thirty-nine east:
right ahead, beyond tanged Salamis, obscured Eleusis—
to port, Cleruchy island.[2]

And now his celestial influence gains:
                    across the atmosphere
                      on the water-sphere
and the wide sinus changes humour and the sea-hues
suffer change
                from Peloponnese Cenchréae
to the homing Attic deck-boy's
own Phaléron.
And suddenly:
                the build of us
                patterns dark the blueing waters

---

[1] See the formula used in questioning the identity of another ship fallen in with at sea.
[2] The island of Aegina.

and shadow-gulls
perch the shadows of the yards across the starboard bow-wave
and on the quiet beam water.

For his chariot
has crossed our course and he stands over Argolis, southward
and westing and darts back his tangent ray.

What bells is that
when the overcast clears on a Mars' Venus-Day
Selene waxed, the sun in the Ram?[1]

Then's when the numbed and scurvied
top-tree boy
grins, like the kouroi[2]
from the straining top-stays:
Up she looms!
three points on the starboard bow.
There's where her spear-flukes
pharos for you
day-star for the sea.
The caulked old triton of us
the master of us
he grins too:
pickled, old, pelagios.
And was it the Lord Poseidon got him
on the Lady of Tyre
queen of the sea-marts
or was his dam in far Colchis abed?
did an Argo's Grogram sire him?

---

[1] See note 1 to page 52 above and see in the account of the Passion according to the three synoptic writers 'darkness over all the earth until the ninth hour'. Cf. page 239 below, text and note 2.
[2] Kouroi, as used of archaic Greek male statues; cf. p. 91 above.

Certain he's part of the olden timbers: watch out for
the run o' the grain on him—look how his ancient knars are
salted and the wounds of the bitter sea on him.

            He's drained it again.

and again they brim it.

Is it the Iacchos

            in his duffle jacket

Ischyros with his sea-boots on?

There's those avers he's wintered with Cronos

under Arctophylax

            out of our *mare*

              into their *See*. [1]

Was it dropped to half gale or did he get it bellyful from
off-shore

            at hurricano strength

cataracted, sulphurous and all

            when he stood into

Leir's river?

            —they say he made Thulê.

Did he hold his course

            mid-sleeve

where, at the wide gusset

            it's thirty-five leagues?[2]

where Môr Iwerddon[3] meets

            Mare Gallicum

where the seas of the islands war with the ocean, to white
            the horse-king's *insulae*

---

[1] Pronounce as in the German *die See* (zay) and so rhyming with *mare* above
and Thule below.

[2] Cf. song *Spanish Ladies*, verse 2.

    'From Ushant to Scilly is thirty-five leagues.'

[3] Môr Iwerddon, Irish Sea, mōrr ee-werr-thon, accent on third syllable.

to blanch
> main and Ushant. [1]

Did Albion put down his screen of brume at:
> forty-nine fifty-seven thirty-four north five twelve four
>> west [2]

to white-out the sea-margin east of northwards to confluent
Fal, and west over Mark's main towards where Trystan's
sands run out to land's last end?
Is that why
> from about forty-nine forty north five twenty west
>> to forty-nine fifty-seven north four-forty west
he sighted no land
> till he first sighted it
a point before the beam in a north-westerly direction
about six leagues
> (by whatever card he knew)
and did he call it
> the Deadman? [3]

Then was when the trestle-tree boy
> from his *thalassa*
across the *mare*, between the Pillars
over the ocean . . .
> a weary time a weary time—
north-way is *Abendsee*—

---

[1] The name of 'Mark', king of Cornwall in the Iseult story, is, in Welsh,
March which means a stallion; the Scilly Isles were part of his domain.

The action of the Atlantic tides meeting the waters of the English Channel is,
I am told, strongly felt along the Breton mainland and around the Island of
Ushant, just as it is on the Cornish side, or much more so.

[2] The bearing of the Lizard Light.

[3] See song *Spanish Ladies*, verse 3:
> 'The first land we made, it is callèd the Deadman'.
> Another version reads:
> 'The first land we sighted was callèd the Dodman'.

        breasting the gulled grey, westing
over wave, wind's daughter
over billow, son of wave.

        Lying to, or going free
before a soldier's wind
        southers nording him
sou'westerlies nor'easting him
        or the blow backs
and easters west him off.
Now (true to a touched stone?)
        north, with the happy veer
and by good management.
Now north by east
        over the nine white grinders
        riding the daughters of the quern of islands[1]
kouroi from over *yr eigion*[2]
        making Dylan's *môroedd*[3]
        holding on towards
Igraine's *dylanau*[4]
        the eyes of her
towards the waters
        of the son of Amblet's daughter.[5]

---

[1] The Scandinavian sea-god Ægir ('sea') was surnamed 'the island mill' and his nine daughters are the waves that grind the rocks or skerries.

[2] *Yr eigion*, the deep (from the Latin, *Oceanus*), pronounce urr ei-gion, accent on first syllable of *eigion*, 'g' hard, ei as in height.

[3] *môroedd*, seas, mōrr-oithe.

[4] *dylanau*, seas, dul-an-ei (as ei in height), accent on middle syllable. This common noun is derived from the proper noun Dylan (dul-an, accent on first syllable). Dylan was the son of the virgin Aranrhod; he took at his birth the nature of the waves.

[5] The name of Arthur's mother in Romance literature is Igraine, the Welsh form is Eigr and *eigr* as a common noun means belle or maiden. She was one of the daughters of Anlawdd Wledig.

Cf. the theory that relates Anlawdd Wledig with Abloyc son of Cunedda Wledig and in turn equates these names with Hamlet prince of Denmark through such forms as e.g. Amlodi, Amblethus, Hamblet. (See Israel Gollancz, *The Sources of Hamlet.*)

What belles she can foam
>   'twixt Uxantis and the Horn![1]
>   And did Morgana's fay-light
abb the warp of mist
>   that diaphanes the creeping ebb, or worse
>   the rapid flow
off Scylla's cisted West-site
>   screening her felspar'd war
with the skerry-mill?[2]
Her menhirs
>   DIS MANIBUS of
>   many a *Schiller's* people
>   many men
>   of many a Clowdisley's ship's company:
for she takes nine
>   in ten!
>   But what Caliban's Lamia
rung him for his Hand of Glory?[3]
(And where the wolf in the quartz'd height
>   —O long long long
before the sea-mark light!—[4]

---

[1] Uxantis is Ushant and the Horn is Cornwall. In Celtic as in Latin *cornu*
meant horn, in modern Welsh *corn*. Hence the Old English compound *Corn-
wealas*, 'the Welsh of the horn'.

[2] Cf. the stone cist discovered in a large barrow on one of the smaller islands
of the Scillies, which whole group is remarkably rich in megalithic burial-sites.
Scilly, as with the Classical Scylla and the common noun 'skerry', means a
rock in the sea.

[3] Cf. as typic of the innumerable losses off the Scillies the two most popularly remembered: In 1875 the *Schiller* whose 300 dead are buried on St
Mary's; in 1707 the flagship and other vessels of the squadron of Sir Clowdisley
Shovell together with 800 men in his ship and himself. Cf. the Scillonian saying
that nine are dead by water for one dead in the course of nature.

Cf. the report that Sir Clowdisley was washed alive to shore but was mur-
dered by a Cornish woman for the jewels on his fingers. Lamia, a land vampire.

[4] Cf. the Wolf Rock Light, between Mount's Bay and the Scillies.

saliva'd the spume
>> over Mark's lost hundred.
Back over
>> the drowned tillage of Leonnoys
>> over the smothered defences
over the hundred and forty *mensae* drowned
in the un-apsed *eglwysau*,[1] under.
Back to the crag-mound
>> in the drowned *coed*
>> under.)[2]

Now nor'-east by north
>> now east by north, easting.
Sou' sou'-west the weather quarter
>> by what slant of wind
they brought her into the Narrow Sea
>> Prydain's *camlas*![3]
that they'll call Mare Austrum[4]
>> *Our* thalassa!
The lead telling fifty in the chops.

---

[1] Latin *mensae*, altars, rhymes with Welsh *eglwysau*, churches; eg-loois-ei, ei as in height, accent on second syllable.

Cf. the identification of the Leonnoys or Lyonesse of Romance literature with the sea-area beyond Land's End; and the independent native Cornish tradition of the submergence of a countryside with the loss of one hundred and forty churches in that area.

[2] Cf. the disputed theory that an old Cornish compound word meaning 'the hoar rock in the wood' is an authentic pre-inundation site-name for the rocky island now called St Michael's Mount.

coed (koid) wood.

[3] Prydain, Britain; prud-ein, ei as in height. *Camlas*, a channel; cam-lass, the 's' is very strongly sibilant, accent on first syllable.

[4] At one period the English Channel was known as 'the South Sea' in Latin MS. See Ordnance Survey Map, *Britain in the Dark Ages*, South Sheet.

Then was when the top-tree boy
from *his* thalassa over their *mare* . . .

                    cried to his towny
before the mast-tree

                    cries louder
(for across the weather)

                    to the man at the steer-tree:
Pretáni-shore![1] Cassitérides!

                    we've rounded their Golden *Cornu*.[2]
Mess-mates of mine

                    we shall be rich men
you shall have y'r warm-dugged Themis
and you, white Phoebe's lune

                    . . . and laughless little Telphousa
what shipman's boy could ask another?
said she'd smile

                    for tin!
What ship's boy would lose her?

                    the skerry-mill rather!
rather the granite molars of the sea-Lamia.

                                   But Albion's brume
begins to thin away, they've made a landfall yet they sight
no Ictian bay and must go a compass.

West now her head

                    she stands scarce six points
off the wind

                    and will that veer?

---

[1] Pronounce pret-tan-ee, accent on middle syllable. The name by which the inhabitants of the British Isles were known to Antiquity before Caesar was the Priteni or the Pretani. Cf. Old Welsh, the *Priten*. It still survives in the Modern Welsh name for the island of Britain itself, Prydain.

[2] The Horn allusion demanded my quite inaccurate 'rounded'.

but no!
                    the smiler draws more south
to rejoice them.
And further souths, till east of south
                as if the Maiden herself
were adjuvant.
                But as that backs
that strengthens . . .
                and for the dissipated brume
the squall-mist and the rain.

Close-cowled, in his mast-head stall the solitary cantor
cups his numbed hand to say his versicle:
                Lánd afóre the beám to stárb'd
one to twó leagues.
And, as the ritual is, the respond is:
                Lánd befóre the beám to stárboard
one to twó leagues.
                But, from the drenched focsle
the stifled murmur is what each heart's wry gloss reads:
                Rock ahead an' shoal to lee
less nor half a Goidel's league!
Is it then
                each brined throat chanties?
We've made from Ilissus
              all the way
matlos of the Maiden
              all the way
              all the way
from Phaléron in the bay

matlos of the Maiden

> all the way b' star and day
> across the *mare*
> over the *See*[1]

to go to Dis in Lear's sea

> matlos of the Maiden

all for thalassócracy
all for thalassócracy

> Maiden help y'r own.

Wot'ld you do with the bleedin' owners?
Wot'ld you do with the bleedin' owners?

> What would you do with 'em?

put 'em in the long boat
put 'em in the long boat

> put them in the wrong boat

and let them sail her

> over the seas to Dis.

Maiden help y'r own
Maiden help y'r own

> Maiden aid us.

Themis, pray.
Phoebe, Telphousa[2]

> pray.

Agelastos Petra

> cleft for us!

Paphia remember us that are indentured to your mother.

---

[1] Pronounced as in *die See*, rhyming with 'day' and '*mare*'.

[2] These names of the three sweethearts of the matelots each connote various aspects of femaleness: the earth, the seasons, the fates, the sibylline art, the menstrual cycle, the moon, so the tides, the huntress, the mother. Telphousa in particular has affinities with Delphi and so with Petra Agelastos. Cf. note 1 to page 56 above.

And us marines, remember us
                    as belong to y'r panzer'd lover.
Sea-wives of Laconia
                    bid your Cytheréa
be mindful of her nativity. ¹
Ladies of Tyre and the Phoenician littoral pray The Lady to
have a native pity on this ship's company—consider: how
many inboard, along of us, belong to *her*!
In all the sun-lands of our cradle-sea
you many that are tutelar
                    regard our anathemata.
Pay our vows Iberian ladies
                    to the Lady of Iberia
for making by her coasts toward this place
we *did call* her by her name:
                    remind her.
In the parts of Liguria about Massilia and at Corbilo-on-Liger,
our last port of call, implore the Three Mothers to recall
what we have donated to all Gallia: almost all, letters most of
all; nor least the love of our Ionian Artemis.
                    Phocaean Huntress, pray for us,
your sea-dogs hunted of the hungry sea. ²

---

¹ Both Paphos on Cyprus and the Island of Cythera off the Laconian coast were
claimed as the place where Aphrodite was delivered from the womb of her
mother, the sea. The nearness of Cyprus to the Syrian coast may indicate a route
by which Es Sitt, The Lady (as they still call her among the Arabs of Palestine),
came to Hellas and so to us.

² Corbilo at the mouth of the Loire was one of the distribution ports of the
tin-traders in pre- and early-historic times. It was from the Phocaean settlement
at Marseilles that Ionian influences infiltrated Gaul, and Phocaean sea-men are
known to have spread the cult of Artemis along the sea-board from Monaco to
Barcelona. The name Marseilles derives from a Phoenician word for 'colony'
and, although in actual historic sequence the Phocaeans displaced the Phoeni-
cians as masters of the sea, in my text I put them in the same boat because they
both were precursors of the Mediterranean thing in the lands of the Western
seaboard.

Vestals of Latium

                    if not yet taught of the Fisherman
give us your suffrage

                     whose lode is the Sea Star.

You that shall spread your hands over the things offered
make *memento* of us
and where the gloss reads *jungit manus*[1] count us among his
argonauts whose argosy you plead,[2] under the sign of the
things you offer.

                     Extend your hands

all you *orantes*

                   for the iron-dark shore
is to our lee
over the lead-dark sea
and schisted Ocrinum looms in fairish visibility
and white-plumed riders shoreward go
                     and
THE BIRDS DECLARE IT
              that wing white and low
that also leeward[3] go
            go leeward to the tor-lands
where the tin-veins maculate the fire-rocks.

---

[1] In the Canon of Mass at the beginning of the prayer *Hanc igitur oblationem*, the rubric directs the priest to spread his hands over the offerings; and after the words 'that we be . . . counted within the flock of thy elect' a further rubric, *Jungit manus*, directs him to join his hands together.

[2] What is pleaded in the Mass is precisely the argosy or voyage of the Redeemer, consisting of his entire sufferings and his death, his conquest of hades, his resurrection and his return in triumph to heaven. It is this that is offered to the Trinity (Cf. 'Myself to myself' as in the *Havamal* is said of Odin) on behalf of us argonauts and of the whole argosy of mankind, and, in some sense, of all sentient being, and, perhaps, of insentient too, for, as Paul says, 'The whole of nature, as we know, groans in a common travail all the while.' (Romans, viii, 22. Knox translation.)

[3] Leeward is to be pronounced lew-ard.

The birds
          have a home
in those rocks.

          Her loosed hair for dog-vane, marking the grain
of the gale, awaiting with confidence her gale-gift, Lamia
waits at her sea-gate, within her land-lair.
Yet his scarfed stem
               furrows the hull's lair
the knee of the head of her
ploughing the grinders
                    white the wash
up over her flare to where her straked sides tumble home.
                    Over her top-strake
green heads inboard rinse her floors to brine her up to her
risings. [1]
O how he cons her!
          the old Pelasgian!
It might be Manannan himself, or the helmsman with the
other *claves*, the gladiatorial vicar of seas. [2]
He yet holds on
          he's weathered Ocrinum
          already he stands on
toward Bolerion. [3]
Drove of world-wind, sun's obedient daughter
               hove down of wind, wave's mother
               pooped of billow, son of wave.

---

[1] Risings (or stringers) are pieces of timber running lengthways of a craft, into which the thwart-boards, on which the rowers sit, are fixed.
[2] Cf. the Keys of Man; the sea-god Manannan (Manawydan) gave his name to that island; bearing also in mind the Keys of the Fisherman with the sword.
[3] Land's End.

Now he stands her in for the isthmus
bearing nor' nor' west three-quarter west.
Shipping a sea
        yet he rounds her to
now are the eyes of her
        due toward her destined haven
        due over the bow-wash
a sky-shaft brights the whited mole
wind-hauled the grinders
        white the darked bay's wide bowl
white echeloned daughters of the island mill
deploy from twenty-fathom water to the inner shoal
spume-blind into the skerry-mill
        he bears on his port of call
distant three leagues and a quarter.

Did he berth her?
        and to schedule?
by the hoar rock in the drowned wood?[1]

*   *   *

[1] See note 2 to page 101 above.

III

ANGLE-LAND

Did he strike soundings off Vecta Insula?
                or was it already the gavelkind *igland*?[1]
Did he lie by
                in the East Road?
was it a kindly *numen* of the Sleeve that headed him clear of
South Sand Head?
Did he shelter in the Small Downs?
Keeping close in, did he feel his way
between the Flats and the Brake?
But, what was her draught, and, what was the ocean doing?
                Did he stand on toward the Gull?
did his second mate sound
                with more than care?
was it perforce or Fortuna's rudder, circumstance or superb
pilotage or clean oblation
                that sheered him from smother
(the unseen necropolis[2] banking to starboard of her).
Or was it she
                Sea-born and Sea-star
whose own, easy and free
                the pious matlos are[3]
or, was it a whim of Poseidon's
(master o' the cinque masters o' lodemanage)[4]

---

[1] When I wrote this I was associating the system of gavelkind with the Isle of Wight solely on account of its being occupied by Jutes, who also occupied Kent, which county is particularly associated with that system and there is evidence of a sort of succession by gavelkind in the Jutish area in Hampshire opposite Wight.

[2] It so happens that it was at Deal, c. 1903, that 'I first beheld the ocean' and I particularly remember that sometimes, in certain conditions of weather and tide, a number of hulks were visible on the Goodwins which then seemed like a graveyard of ships.

[3] Cf. Archbishop David Mathew, *British Seamen*, p. 48, 'Easy and gallant they defend the freedom of the seas and the shores of England'. And cf. song, *All the Nice Girls Love a Sailor*, line 5, 'Bright and breezy, free and easy'.

[4] 'Cinque' and 'lodemanage' to be said as in English, indeed as in Cockney English. (Each of the Cinque Ports had a pilot called the Master of Lodemanage.)

whose own the Island's approaches are
>>>> that kept her?
Was the Foreland?
>>>> was the Elbow?
under fog.
>>> He might have been deeped in the Oaze![1]
Or
>>> by the brumous numen drawn on
or
>>> in preclear visibility
by the invisible wind laboured
it might have been Dogger or Well
>>> to bank her a mound
without a sheet to wrap her
without a shroud to her broken back.
>>>> Past where they placed their *ingas*-names
where they speed the coulter deep
>>>> in the open Engel fields
to this day.
>>>>> How many poles
of their broad Angle hidage
to the small scattered plots, to the lightly furrowed *erwau*,[2]
that once did quilt Boudícca's róyal *gwely*?[3]

Past where they urn'd their calcined dead from Schleswig
over the foam.

---

[1] Cf. Oaze Deep, an area of water so named in the mouth of the Thames.

[2] *Erwau*, plural of *erw*, acre; érr-wye (err as in the Latin *errare*), accent on first syllable. Not in fact an acre or any fixed unit, but land equally divided among the members of a plough-team under the Celtic system of co-aration.

[3] *gwely*, gwel-ly, bed, but also used of the collective lands of a group. Typical Celtic ploughing was less deep than that of subsequent invaders.

(Close the south-west wall of the chester, without the orbit,
if but a stone's throw: you don't want to raise an Icenian
Venta's Brettisc¹ ghost.
He'll latin-runes tellan in his horror-coat standing:
IAM REDIT ROMA
                    his lifted palm his VERBVM is.)

Past where the ancra-man, deeping his holy rule
in the fiendish marsh
                    at the *Geisterstunde*
                    on *Calangaeaf* night²
heard the bogle-*baragouinage*.
                    Crowland-*diawliaidd*³
Waelisc-man lingo speaking?
                    or Britto-Romani gone *diaboli*?
or Romanity gone *Waelisc*?⁴
Is Marianus wild Meirion?⁵
is Sylvánus
                    Urbigéna's son?
has toga'd Rhufon⁶
                    (gone Actáeon)
come away to the Wake
                    in the bittern's low aery?
along with his towny

---

¹ Pronounce bret-tish.
² *Calangaeaf*, Winter Calands, November 1, cal-lan-gei-av, accent on ei
pronounced as in height.
³ *diawliaidd*, devils, deeowl-yithe, accent on first syllable. The Mercian
saint, Guthlac, when an anchorite on Crowland island in the Fens, hearing the
speech of surviving Britons thought it the language of devils.
⁴ Pronounce wye-lish.
⁵ The Roman name Marianus gave Meirion in Welsh; hence 'Merioneth'.
⁶ Rhufon, rhiv-von, Romanus. Urbigena; cf. Urbgen in Nennius, Urien in
the Romances. The late Gilbert Sheldon wrote: 'The Latin name *Urbigena*,
city-born, is disguised as Urien'. Pronounce as urr-bee-gain-ah, accent on gain.

Patricius gone the *wilde Jäger*?

From the *fora*
              to the forests.
Out from *gens Romulum*
         into the *Weal*-kin[1]
dinas-man gone *aethwlad*[2]
cives gone wold-men
                 . . . from Lindum to London
bridges broken down.

What was his *Hausname*?
         he whose North Holstein urn
they sealed against the seep of the Yare?
If there are *Wealas*[3] yet
                 in the Waltons
what's the cephalic index of the *môrforynion*,[4] who knell
the bell, who thread the pearls that were Ned Mizzen's eyes,
at the five fathom line off the Naze?
         On past the low low lands of the Holland that
Welland winds to the Deepings north of the Soke
past where Woden's gang *is gens Julia* for Wuffingas new to
old Nene and up with the Lark[5]
past the south hams and the north tons

---

[1] Cf. *Wealcyn* used by the Teutonic invaders of any group of kindred within
those lands which had been part of Roman Britain. Pronounce, wa-ahl.

[2] *dinas*, city, din-ass, accent on first syllable.
aethwlad, outlaw, aeth-oolahd, ae as ah +eh, accent on first syllable.

[3] *Wealas*, wa-ahl-ass, plural of *Wealh*, a Welshman.

[4] *môrforynion*, water-maidens, mōrr-vorr-un-yon, accent on third syllable.

[5] The Wuffingas, that during the fifth-century invasions made settlements in
the Fen Country, through which flow the Nene and the Lark, seem later on to
have claimed descent from both Odin and Caesar.

past the weathered thorps and
                         the Thorpe
that bore, that bred
                         him whom Nike did bear
her tears at flood
and over the scatter of the forebrace bitts
                         down to the orlop
at twenty five minutes after one of the clock
in the afternoon, on a Monday
twelve days before the Calends of November
outside the Pillars
                    where they closed like a forest
                         . . . in 13 fathoms' water
unanchored in the worsening weather. [1]
                                   Far drawn on away
from the island's field-floor, upwards of a hundred fathoms
over where, beyond where, in the fifties, toward the sixties,
north latitude
                              all our easting waters
are confluent with the fathering river and tributary to him:
where Tamesis, Great Ouse, Tyne from the Wall's end, demarking Tweed, Forth that winds the middle march, Tummel
and wide looping Tay (that laps the wading files when Birnam
boughs deploy toward Dunsinane—out toward the Goat
Flats).

---

[1] See Collingwood's dispatch to the Admiralty Lords as reported in a con-
temporary edition of *The Times*, giving particulars of the action on Monday,
October 21, 1805, and also James, *Naval History*, Vol. IV, 1837 edtn.
  'Seeing by the direction of her course that the Victory was about to follow
the example of the Royal-Sovereign, the French and Spanish ships ahead of the
British weather column closed like a forest.' p. 38.
  'To add to the perilous condition of the British fleet and prizes, the ships
were then in 13 fathoms' water, with the shoals of Trafalgar but a few miles to
leeward.' p. 87.

Spey of the Symbol stones and Ness from the serpentine mere
all mingle Rhenus-flow
                              and are oned with him
in Cronos-*meer*.
I speak of before the whale-roads or the keel-paths were from
Orcades to the fiord-havens, or the greyed green wastes that
they strictly grid
quadrate and number on the sea-green *Quadratkarte*
                              one eight six one G
                              for the fratricides
of the latter-day, from east-shore of Iceland
bis Norwegen[1]
(O Balin O Balan![2]
                    how blood you both
the *Brudersee*
                    toward the last pháse
of our dear West.)

*   *   *

[1] I had in mind a squared chart issued for special service requirements by the
German Naval Command, described as *Europäisches Nordmeer. Ostküste von Island
bis Norwegen, 1861 G.*, on which the grid, numerals and other markings are
imposed in green on a large-scale map of that area. Date *c.* 1940.
[2] Cf. Malory Bk. II, Cp. 18. How Balin met with his brother Balan and
how each slew other unknown.

IV
REDRIFF

Or

  did he make the estuary?
was the Cant smiling
  and the Knock smooth?
Did our Tidal Father bear him
     by Lower Hope to Half Reach?
Did he berth in the Greenland or was she moored
in the Pool?
Did he tie up across the water
     or did she toss at the Surrey shore?
Had he business at Dockhead?
Did he sign Tom Bowline on:
    ord-in-ary-seaman
in place of the drownded Syro-Phoenician?
Did he bespeak

    of Eb Bradshaw, Princes Stair:
listed replacement of sheaves to the running-blocks, new
dead-eyes to the standing shrouds, some spare hearts for the
stays, a heavy repair in the chains, some nice work up at
the hound

       . . . would he expedite.
It 'ld be well worth his while—for a tidy consideration
could she have preference—for she must weigh on time or
the dues 'ld ruin 'em—would he, for once, oil an elbow—
would he please to hustle the job—and not so over nice with
the finish.
Not for a gratis load of the sound teak in
Breaker's Yard

    and that we could well do with.
Not for a dozen cords of Norweyan, red nor yaller, paid for,
carried and stacked.
Not for a choice of the best float of Oregon in the mast-pond.
Not for as many cubic fathoms of best Indies lignum vitae

as 'ld stock us till we re-sheave the blocks for master-
bargees plying the Styx.
Not for a pickin' of all the bonded stuffs passed over the
quays in a full working week between the Bridge and Battlebridge Stairs[1]
                                and there's a tidy jorum
to pile a mint in sterling—to rig out Ann my wife like Suky
Tawdry.
Not at the price of half the freights, felled of the living wood,
a lent o' tides, brings to all the wharves, from here round to
the Royal Vi't'lin', when Proserpine unbinds the Baltic.[2]
Not if he signed me fair a note of hand for all the gold on his
fleece.
Nor for this port's authorities
                                and I'm a citizen.
Not if the Trinity Brethren
                                and Clemens himself[3]
stood caps in hand for a month of Sundays
                                and them I must needs respect.
Not if the Holy Ghost made ready to blow on his mainsail.
Nor for a boozed Murphy's bull in curial-cursive and leaded
from the scarlet pontiff o' the West.
And, as for next Thor's Day's night tide
                                tell the Wop, to-go-to
                                                Canute

---

[1] That is to say on the Surrey shore between London Bridge and the water-
stairs called Battlebridge Stairs east of Hays Wharf. Warehouses set aside for
goods in bond being situated between these two points.

[2] The Rotherhithe timber-trade was particularly brisk in the spring when the
ice melted and freed the ships in the Baltic. The victualling yard is at Deptford.

[3] St Clement of Alexandria is the patron saint of Trinity House—because of
the Pharos at Alexandria? I do not know, perhaps some reader may.

if he can find him
          down at the Galley Wall [1]
(though he's many times before *his* time).
But tell him:

          we scamp no repairs here; no botched Riga
deal nor wood that's all American, softs nor hards, hewn or
sawn, heart n'r sap, cis- or trans- Gangem-land teak, or fair-
grained *ulmus* from sylvan wester lands or goodish East Mark
oak via Fiume in British bottoms
                              let alone
heart of island-grown
          seasoned in m' neighbour's yard
leaves this bench.
But
     tell him
tell him from me
          if he waits his turn an' damps down his Sicily
sulphur [2] we'll spokeshave those deadeyes for him as smooth
as a *peach* of a cheek
          we'll fay that hounding trim and proper—and of
the best spruce, [3] to rhyme with her mainmast, we'll square

---

[1] The allusion is to the Galley Wall Road district in Rotherhithe. The name
is associated locally with an event described in *The Anglo-Saxon Chronicle*, under
the year 1016: 'Then came the ships to Greenwich and within a little space
they went to London and they dug a great ditch on the south side and dragged
their ships to the west side of the bridge. . . .' (trans. Bohn edtn 1849). This
association between Canute's galleys and this street-name was, at all events, the
popular tradition in my mother's girlhood (in the late eighteen-seventies) and
was the opinion of Canon Beck of Rotherhithe church. 'Canute's Ditch', as it
was called, was believed to run from near where Greenland Dock now is and to
join the Thames again in Walworth: its actual siting is disputed.

[2] Apart from timber from the Baltic and elsewhere, the Rotherhithe docks
in the last century received large cargoes of sulphur from Palermo and other
Mediterranean ports.

[3] Cf. 'a nyew mayne mast of spruce with a nyew staye hounsyd and skarvyd
with the same wood whyche mast ys of length from the Hounse to the step
25 yards' (1532) O.E.D., under 'hound'.

true and round to a nicety the double piercin's o' that cap—
and of keel-elm.

      If he leaves it to us
we'll fix him dandy.
But tell him—with respects from me
tell him—tell the old Jason:

      As sure as I was articled, had I the job of mortisin'
the beams to which was lashed and roved the Fault in all of
us, I'ld take m' time and set that aspen transom square to
the Rootless Tree

      or dash m' buttons!

               . . . he's got
till the Day o' Doom
to sail the bitter seas o' the world!

*   *   *

V

THE LADY OF THE POOL

THE LADY OF THE POOL

Did he meet Lud at the Fleet Gate? did he count the top-
trees in the anchored forest of Llefelys
                                        under the White Mount?[1]

Did ever he walk the twenty-six wards of the city, within
and extra, did he cast his nautic eye on her
                                        clere and lusty under kell[2]
in the troia'd lanes of the city?
And was it but a month and less from the septimal month,
and did he hear, seemly intuned in *East-Seaxna*-nasal[3]
            (whose nestle-cock *polis* but theirs knows the sweet
gag and in what *urbs* would he hear it if not in Belin's
oppidum, the greatest *burh* in nordlands?)[4]

---

[1] Cf. the tale Lludd and Llefelys (lle-vél-iss), a legend concerning 'King
Lud' and his brother in which occurs the assembling of vessels in the Pool
of London. The White Mount=The Tower in Welsh tales.

[2] Cf. Dunbar *In Honour of the City of London*, v. 6:
            'Fair be thy wives, right lovesom white and small
            Clere be thy virgins, lusty under kellis'

[3] *East-Seaxna*, 'of the East Saxons', pronounce a-ahst sa-ahx-nah. Cf. the
theory that the cockney intonation derives from that of the English people of
Essex; London being their capital just as it was associated with the Trinobantian
Britons before them, whose tribal commune Caesar referred to as *civitas
Trinobantum*. In this factual community-name we have the origin of the legendary
city of Trinovantum, or Troy Novant, which the work of Geoffrey of Monmouth made an integral part of our national mythological deposit, whereby,
through the Trojan, Brute, of the line of Aeneas, Venus and Jove, our tradition
is linked with all that that succession can be made to signify; and seeing what
we owe to all that, the myth proposes for our acceptance a truth more real than
the historic facts alone discover.

[4] Cf. the *Ragnar Lodbrok Saga*
'Lundunaborg which is the greatest and the most famous of all the burhs in
the northern lands.'

Who'll try my sweet prime lavendula
I cry my introit in a Dirige-*time*
Come buy for summer's weeds, threnodic stalks
For in Jane's ditch Jack soon shall white his earliest rime[1]

Come, come buy

good for a ditty-box, my fish-eye
good to sweeten y'r poop-bower, cap'n.
Come buy

or else y'r duck'ill cry.
Come buy my sweet lavender

that bodes the fall-gale westerlies
and ice on slow old Baldpate[2]

when the Nore gulls fly this way that tell to Lear's
river a long winter's tale.

Was already rawish crost the Lower Pool[3] afore four o'
the clock this fine summer mornin'—it might 've been
Lemon's Day.[4] An' cuckoo seeming but bare flown and
Ember Ides not yet by a long way come, in pontiff Juliuses
'versal colander and them not yet sung their Crouchmasses[5]

---

[1] When, in August, lavender was cried in the street, my maternal grand-mother was saddened by the call, because she said it meant that summer was almost gone and that winter was again near. Cf. also the vulgar tradition which wrongly derived the district-name Shoreditch from Jane Shore who was believed to have died in, or been cast into, a ditch in that vicinity. It may not be without relevance to note that lavender, though perhaps particularly associated with eighteenth- and nineteenth-century London, was cultivated at Hitchin in Hert-fordshire in the sixteenth century; also that it was used by the *meddygon*, phy-sicians, in thirteenth-century tribal Wales. It was considered efficacious for disorders of the brain and of the nervous system. It is said to please lions.

[2] Cf. *Oranges and Lemons*:

'Old father bald-pate
Say the slow bells of Aldgate.'

[3] The bend of the river by Rotherhithe and Shadwell.

[4] November 23, St Clement of Alexandria,
Cf.   'Oranges and Lemons
Say the bells of St Clemens'

[5] Feast of the Exaltation of the Cross, September 14, see note 3 to page 165 below.

1 Cf. the *Black Book of the Exchequer* and the ecclesiastical *Ordo* books which together provide a cross-check on dates of events when there was no universal method of dating but many local uses.

2 St Mary Whitechapel.

3 St Bride's, Fleet Street and the Bridewell. Cf. the association of Bride or Brigit with candles and fire as in her shrines at Kildare and elsewhere.

4 All Hallows, London Wall, was at the City's farthest extent north from the river-front.

5 Houndsditch; the Vicinal Way entered Roman London at Aldgate.

6 Cf. Apocalypse xii, 2.

7 It is important to recall that the site of London consisted of two hills separated by a wide stream (the Walbrook), that the Fleet and waters running into it skirted the west side, that the whole site was well watered with springs and that, like Rome, London was famous for its fresh water. The early accounts of the city suggest that the wells, rills, shares, bourns, streamlets, ponds, apart from the great tidal river, impressed the imagination of the writers.

8 St Martin's, near Cheapside, called Martin Pomary, whether for a proper name or from an orchard or from the *pomoerium* of the Roman city has been much debated.

9 St Michael, Cornhill. Marmor, an earlier form of Mars, who was a god of corn as well as, or rather before, he was, like Michael, a leader of armies.

10 St Mary-at-Hill from which the city lanes sloped down to the wharves of Billingsgate. This district was called 'Romeland'; another 'Romeland' was around the Dowgate, where Cannon Street Station now is.

11 Mary le Bow and Mary Aldermary. The latter was so called because it was the oldest site dedicated to our Lady in London; the former, by way of contrast, was known as Mary Newchurch. Crepel, covered or arched way. Cf. cripple-gap, and (U.S.) cripple, a supporting framework.

12 The discovery of skulls and other bones of oxen under St Paul's in 1316 assisted a traditional belief that the site had been sacred to Iuppiter, or Diana. On the feast of the Commemoration of St Paul, June 30, the dean and chapter, zoomorphically vested and crowned with roses, received a buck from the deer-park of Curingham in Essex; the animal was oblated and put to death; then the antlered head was carried in procession to the west door, where a forester 'blowed the death of the buck'.

13 St Stephen-super-Walbrook, the church of Stephen, deacon and first martyr, originally stood on the west bank of the brook and literally 'upon' it; its present site is much farther east.

14 St Mary Woolnoth; properly called St Mary of the Nativity, in Langbourn Ward. 'So-called,' says Stow, 'of a long bourne of sweet water which of old time . . . ran down to the west end of St Mary Woolnoth church . . . breaking into small shares, rills and streams.'

by tax-chandler's Black Exchecky Book[1] nor yet thumbed
Archie's piscopal *Ordo* to figure out the moon of it.

From the Two Sticks an' a' Apple [2] to Bride o'
the Shandies' Well[3] over the Fleet; from Hallows-on-Wall to
the keel-haws[4] ; from the ditch without the Vicinal Gate[5] to
Lud's hill; within and extra the fending circuit, both banks
the wide and demarking middle-brook that waters, from the
midst of the street of it,[6] our twin-hilled Urbs[7]. At Martin
miles in the Pomarary[8] (where the Roman pippins grow) at
winged Marmor *miles*,[9] gilt-lorica'd on his wheat-hill, stick-
ing the Laidly Worm as threats to coil us all.

At the Lady-at-Hill
above Romeland's wharf-lanes[10]
at the Great Mother's newer *chapelle*
at New Heva's Old Crepel.[11]

(Chthonic *matres* under the croft:
springan a Maye's *Aves* to clerestories.

Delphi in sub-crypt:
luce flowers to steeple.)

At Paul's
and faiths under Paul
where

so Iuppiter me succour!
they do garland them with Roman roses and do have stitched
on their zoomorphic apparels and vest 'em gay for Artemis.

When is brought in her stag to be pierced,
when is bowed his meek head between the porch and the
altar, when is blowed his sweet death at the great door, on the
day before the calends o' Quintilis.[12]

At the tunicled martyr's[13]
from where prills the seeding under-stream.

At Mary of the Birth[14]
by her long bourn of sweet water.

In where she mothers

[127]

her painters an' limners. [1]

        In Pellipar's

where she's *virgo inter virgines*

for the skinner's boys an' budge-dressers. [2]

        In all the memorials

of her buxom will

            (what brought us ransom, captain!)

as do renown our city. [3]

She's as she of Aulis, [4] master:

not a puff of wind without her!

her fiat is our fortune, sir: like Helen's face

'twas that as launched the ship. [5]

              Or may I never

keep company more with a dunce of a maudlin inceptor—

though he were a seraph for sub-distinctions.

                . . . did black deth

---

[1] St Mary Staining, Cripplegate, was believed to be so named on account of the painter-stainers whose workshops were in that vicinity; but it may more likely derive from the place name, Stains.

[2] St Mary Pellipar, Lime Street, so called after the skin-dressers that worked in the locality (*pellio* a furrier). The proper name of the church is St Mary, St Ursula and the Eleven Thousand Virgins.

[3] Cf. *Twelfth Night*, III, 3.

[4] It will be recalled that the expedition to Troy was becalmed in Aulis harbour because the vow concerning Iphigenia was not fulfilled.

[5] Though 'Minerva springs eternally from the head of Jove', the Eternally Begotten could not have become begotten on a creature except by a creature's pliant will. It is significant that in masses of the Common of our Lady the gospel chosen by the church is Luke XI, 27-28, where Jesus leaves no doubt that the blessedness of his mother resides firstly in the compliancy of her will.

Since writing the above note there has now (1951) been published a sermon on the Assumption, by Aelred of Rievaulx, in which that twelfth-century English saint observes that Mary was 'doubtless blessed in receiving the Son of God bodily into her womb, but she was much more blessed for first receiving him in her mind and heart'. He goes on to say that but for Mary's acceptance the gospel could never have been preached. Which Irenaeus, in second-century Gaul, had expressed when he said 'She was constituted the cause of our salvation'.

have him young? Or does he sit degreed an' silked in oriel'd halls, in a cure o' Christ and shorn to sign it, warming their disputations till frigid syllogism pulses like mother nature —by a most exact art?

Oh! do the budged owls pluck where their forelocks were, as did remunerated errand boys—when manners was —for proper admiration to see divine science by the muse so fired?

Is their chilly curia a very thalamos: is Lady Verity with Poesy now wed, and at that bed, by Prudentia curtained close, does the Trivium curtsy and does each take hand and to the Quadrivium call: Music! for a saraband?[1]

And does serene Astronomy carry the tonic *Ave* to the created spheres, does old Averroes show a leg?[2]—for what's the song b' Seine and Isis determines toons in caelian consistories—or so this cock-clerk[3] once said.

Do all in *aula* rise
and cede him his hypothesis:

Mother is requisite to son?
Or would they have none
                    of his *theosis*?
He were a one for what's due her, captain.
Being ever a one for what's due *us*, captain.
He knew his Austin![4]

                                        But he were ever
at his distinctions, captain.
They come—and they go, captain.

---

[1] Cf. the division of the Seven Liberal Arts into the Trivium: Grammar Dialectic, Rhetoric; and the Quadrivium: Arithmetic, Geometry, Astronomy, Music.

[2] He held matter to be uncreate and from all eternity.

[3] Pronounce to rhyme with 'lurk'.

[4] Cf. Augustine, 'God became man that man might become god.'

At Sepulchre's Turnagain Lane, t'ward the Smooth-field pond, beyond the New Gate[1]

what were lime-bonded Kentish rag and Surrey tile at the beginning of the Sixth Age o' the World—or, by Janus, I weren't a freestone-mason's paramour nor him not 'dentured proper in his Mystery: him sweared as it were work o' Roma,—what he spelled-out *backward*, captain.

And once, captain, on a showery night's fall in the thunder-nones of hot July, m' apricots big in the convent apron and the pretty gilly-flower to pink the white of his mason's paper hat; the Hammerer's summer-flashers from time to time and far off over the Arx of Julius, and nearer by and now and again brighted up old imaged Lud, as some tell is 'balmed 'Wallon, high-horsed above Martin *miles*,[2] what the drovers pray to, full of our London ales and their 'Gomery fables.

Inclined against these shadowy courses, close-in, under the lower string-course, next the dark hunch of the gate. From the dripping impost the gusted drops moisted the ransom'd flesh of both of us—from the *right* side of the gate, cap-tin.   The runnels brimmed so, was a marvel if the blessèd guardian head, cisted under, that keeps Lud's town, weren't down stream with dogs and garbage an' such poor Tibs as had come to the ninth death b' water.

In this wild eve's thunder-rain, at the batement of it, the night-shades now much more come on: when's the cool,

---

[1] This gate, alone of all the gate-sites of Roman London, has yielded positive material evidence of Roman gate-work.

[2] Cf. the story popularized by Geoffrey of Monmouth that King Cadwallon was embalmed and set in brass armour on a brass horse 'over the West Gate of London' (in this case not Newgate but Ludgate) and that St Martin, Ludgate Hill, was built for his requiems. See Geoffrey of Monmouth *History of the Kings of Britain*, Bk. XII, cp. 13. Altogether apart from this legendary account it is documented that images in fact adorned Ludgate in the medieval period; the 'images of Lud and other kings' being repaired or added in 1260.

even, after-light. When lime-dressed walls, petals on stalks,
a kerchief, a shift's hem or such like, and the Eve's white of
us . . . *and* cap-tin, the bleached hemp of a fore-brace, the
white of the wake beyond the dead-water, or the fresh paint-
work, for'ard, eh? captain, looms up curiously exact and
clear, more real by half than in the busy light as noses everywhere at stare-faced noon—more real . . . but more of
Faëry by a long chalk.

An' in this transfiguring after-clarity he seemed to call me
his . . . Fl - ora . . . *Flora Dea*[1] he says . . . whether to me or
into the darks of the old ragstone courses?

. . . how are you for conundrums, captain?

And again, once in especial,
at a swelt'rin' close August day's close, three sultry eves
after they sing *Gaudeamus*[2]—on m' own name-day captain,
on the of the British Elen that found the Wood[3]—Ceres big
moon half ris beyond her own Cornhill, behind de Arcubus as

---

[1] It has been said that the name of the goddess Flora was used as a mystical
or secret name for Rome.

[2] Cf. the introit for the mass of the Assumption, August 15, '*Gaudeamus omnes
in Domino*', etc.

[3] Flavia Julia Helena, wife of Constantius Chlorus and mother of Constantine
the Great, associated in the Christian calendar with the tradition of the finding
of the Wood of the Cross. In certain dioceses of England, her feast, August 18,
takes precedence and is celebrated with a special mass and office. Breviaries and
missals used to assert that she was born in Britain but this has now (1949) been
corrected to Drepanum in Asia Minor. Apart from her importance in the Christian tradition as St Helen, and her eminence as Empress, there has gathered
around her a separate secular body of legend of much beauty but of exceptional
contradiction and tangle deriving from Welsh sources. In these tales she is
variously the daughter of King Cole, of Eudaf of Arfon, of Eudav of Cornwall,
the Roman roads in Wales bear her name, she is wife of Constantius, she is the
wife of Macsen Wledig (Maximus), she is Helen of the Hosts, she is builder of
the Wall of London; it was as hard to look upon her because of her beauty as it
is to look upon the sun when brightest, and so on. In these stories she takes on
something of her classical namesake and stands for the beauty of Britain beguiling
the emperor and directing the power-struggles; her family conquer Rome for
Maximus, she is indeed almost Britannia herself. Not so often has one historic
person gathered to herself such a diversity of significances. She can be seen in
the tradition of religion to be the mother who gave birth to the 'Peace of the

chimes *I do not know*,[1] at the same 'buttment of the guard-house wall, the day-guard dismissed, the sergeant and his crawlers do the small beer play at dice, within; the new-posted first night-relief already a-nodding over his sloped stock—already a-bed with the Queen o' Cockayne—or, champion in the stour he'd fled . . .

> thank God
we've got the lightermen, captain!

    Between the heats and the cool, at day's ebb and night-flow, the lode already over the fen of Islington, pressed we was to the same cranny of the wall to right of the same 'brassure of the same right gate-jamb—so Janus save me, but bodies will. The whitest of the Wanderers, what was Julius Caesar's mother, white over toward Bride's Well, and this her fish day—and again he says it, but this time it's *Bona Dea*[2] he cries . . . Hills o' the Mother he says, an' y'r lavender, the purple, he says, an' then he says, but more slow:

> Roma aurea Roma[3]

Roma . . . amor, amor . . . Roma. Roma, wot's in the feminine[4] gender, he says.

Church', the Woman through whom Cross and Vexillum become one; and in our native (Welsh) secular tradition she may perhaps have become identified with other matriarchal figures of unknown antiquity; and, because of being the wife of Constantius, she shared something of his traditional role as restorer and orderer in Britain. The two traditions together envisage the fusion of typic figures of great splendour and depth: *imperatrix* plus numinous 'beauty' plus Holy Woman. The epistle at her mass is, very happily, *Mulierem fortem quis inveniet?* (Proverbs XXXI, 10-31). She is here envisaged as Holy Wisdom.

  [1] Cf. 'I do not know, says the great bell of Bow'. Bow Church, Maria de Arcubus.

  [2] Cf. the female guardian deity of Rome, essentially oracular and representing the whole female principle, the mother-sister-wife of Faunus, her male counterpart.

  [3] Cf. *Roma caput orbis splendor spes aurea Roma*. The inscription, now lost, that Leo IV (Pope 847-855) put over the gate of the wall which he built around the extension of the city on the right bank of the Tiber. See Nicolette Gray, *The Paleography of Latin Inscriptions in the Eighth, Ninth and Tenth Centuries in Italy*.

  [4] Cf. the eighteenth-century rhyme 'Amo, amas, I love a lass her form is tall and slender, etc.', ending with 'in the nominative case and in the feminine gender'. Feminine to rhyme with 'fine'.

What rogue's cant is this? I said. Whereas, inly, I for love languished.

                    And after a bit—his left hand was under my head, captain, and with his right that did embrace me,[1] he touched, his palm open, the courses of the wall, the back of his hand to the freestone face—as if he marked the holy 'Vangelium for a clerk to kiss,[2] as if he *read* the wall, captain, and says: Augusta . . . Augusta Trinobantum; and then asks, You was Essex bred? No, I said, I were reared on the Surrey side though native within Aldgate.[3] Sanfairyann he says and goes straight on: When I were a young man in France impressed for service in Artois an' drafted to Ordnance, an ingeniator out o' Burgundy, but a Breton b' birth, tells me that at Augustodunum, the great works there, was, in times far far back, reared of men, like those of my mob, from Kent, and how from the provinces of this island came the best artists in those days.[4]

---

[1] Cf.
                    '. . . quia amore langueo
                    Laeva ejus sub capite meo
                    et dextera illius amplexabitur me.'
                                        Song of Songs II, 5-6.

[2] At the commencement of the Gospel it is the business of the assistant to mark the passage to be read by the minister. This he does by placing the tips of his fingers, his palm open and upwards, at the initial words of that passage. At the conclusion of the Gospel the minister kisses the open book.

[3] Ammianus Marcellinus, in the fourth century, says of London, that though it was called by the ancients Londinium, it was in his day called 'Augusta'.

Londinium was honoured with the title of Augusta in the age of Theodosius the Great and it was Augusta of the Trinobantes, that is to say it remained the capital of the people of Essex and Middlesex as well as being the chief city of Britain. The Essex connection survived the Anglo-Saxon conquest, as Bede, writing in 700, and as an Englishman, explicitly states that London is a town of the people of Essex.

[4] Eumenius, a rhetorician writing in Augustodunum (Autun in Burgundy) in the late third century, says that for the repairing of that city, masons were brought from the Provinces of Britain because skilled workmen were to be had there in large numbers.

Yes? I said, but not carping like nor crossing him—best let
him rehearse his tale awhile seeing as it touched his service
oversea—they all be apt at their rehearsals, captain, what
was upon a time and long since within far sound of a bombard,
captain.

But then it seemed he would be addressed, not to me
at all, but, sort of, to the formless airs

again his hand the while a-fondle-ing the wall—as
might the hand of the blind—but with open eye, as seemed
aligned toward where the keels tie up below Fleet Bridge.

And then, as if he perceive a body—coming
as if he hails a personage

where was but insentience
and baulk of stone

he sings out and clear:

REDDITOR LVCIS ÆTERNÆ[1]

These, captain, were his precisive words—what sentiments I
can't construe—but at which, captain, I cried: Enough!

Let's to terrestrial flesh, or
bid good-night, I thought.

---

[1] 'Restorer of the Eternal Light'; this is inscribed on a gold medallion found
at Beauvains near Arras (an area rich in memories for many of us), struck to
commemorate the relief of London in AD 296 by Constantius Chlorus, the hus-
band of St Helena (see page 131 above, note 3). He is mounted and with a lance,
his horse stepping from the gang-plank of a boat at a turreted gateway inscribed
LON. where a female figure kneels with welcoming arms. The words *Redditor
etc.* are inscribed above the figure of the emperor. Although this may but commemorate a chance victory in a war of rival generals, none the less Constantius,
at that moment, was the outward sign of something and was himself the implement of what he signified, namely: in the domain of accidental fact, the saving of
London from immediate sack; in the domain of contemporary politics, the
restoration of Britain to unity with the West, and in the domain of perennial
idea, the return to Britain of the light of civilization. I have adopted the suggestion of one writer that the gate and the water on the medallion may represent
Ludgate and the Fleet River; the latter being tidal, and navigable for long after
Roman times.

I said, I'm unversed, I said,
nor a clerk of nigromantics, though for a short while put to
school in a sisterhood,[1] and know the ample shape of our
Redemption, and could answer up, and before the Ordinary,
when he put on us the Second Indelible Mark.

But am a simple person,
sponsored in Papeys-in-Wall,[2] but reared up by Redriff
mast-pond; swaddled, crawled and found my walking legs in
a keel-haw, did know a sheaved block from a dead-eye before
I were gunwhale high, knowed the lily i' the shipman's card
before any water-boy made for to know me.

Learned much of the dear God's created
orbis from such as navigate and circumnavigate
      from tarpaulins and salts, clerks of nautics
that thither from the known to the knowable
and hither again to haven
whose first premiss, main-stay and Last Gospel is: That the
Lode be constant[3]

                    yet dealing much
in the peregrinations of Venus.
Much have I learned of them.

As him, the skipper of the *Margaron*, sister-ship to
the *Troy Queen*, but slighter entranced, and in the water is
the wilder swan:

---

[1] Clerk, pronounce to rhyme with 'lurk'; and cf. 'And the thyrd syster,
Morgan le Fey, was put to scole in a nonnery, and ther she lerned so moche that
she was a grete clerke of nygromancye.' *Malory*, Bk. I, Ch. 2.

[2] See above 'native within Aldgate'. Papey Church was in that Ward.

[3] The importance to the medieval seaman of the Pole Star, which they called
Stella Maris, is appreciated by recalling that until the sixteenth century their
manuals of seamanship were entitled *The Regiment of the North Star*.

the finer the scantlings

the harder to con!

Was him that shipped
the bull narwhal off Thor's own haven in Faëry[1] an' palm-off
the single ivory for genu-ine Helyon unicorn[2] on the con-
juror-doctors as laces their draughts of Cam with noggins of
sibylline Deva.

As take
dilute essence of the best Ionic anaximanders and shake in
some well merlin'd extract of vergil.

As him that does the hor'scopes
and tinctures various his potions of innocent water for the
vomits and creaturely swellings of them of the curia, up
stream. A very John-on-Patmos for uncoverings and all
rombuses, vaticinations an' anagrams; as see the apotheosis
of imperium in a cloud of his own bottled smoke, under the
form of a woman clothed with the sea, head-armoured like a
Troian-Greek and in her fist the tree of a fish-spear.[3]

But, he were had
on that sea-tusker.

---

[1] The port of Thorshavn in the Faroe Islands; and cf. the idea that the Welsh
Otherworld (*annwfyn*) is to be associated with those islands.

[2] John of Hess, a medieval itinerary-writer, in reporting that unicorns were
to be found east of the Red Sea where Moses made the bitter waters sweet,
names that place 'the fields of Helyon'.

[3] The pre-application here of some of the activities associated later with the
mathematician John Dee (Foundation Fellow of Trinity, Cambridge, physician
and astrologer to Elizabeth and credited with employing adverse magic to secure
the death of her predecessor) is on account of his being, *par excellence*, typic of
persons with Merlinesque pretensions, such as the nineteenth century Dr Price,
of Llantrisant. Dee has also been credited with originating the use of the term
'British Empire'. He was a Londoner, but, one presumes, not without consan-
guinity with the countrymen of the Tudors.

Or him from Aleppo come
the master o' the *Mary*.

Wot a tiger! His beard full of gale.

Overdue a nine month, writ-off for lost bottomry by the brokers long since, loanees and loaners as much in charity as a Tib and a Towser . . .

but not a loss
and fetching it, though by hollow seas tossed and laboured of hard blows from every point of the card.

Making it:
one morning, very early, on the second day of the week at the rising, the dawn began but whiles it were yet but darkish —they would 'a' said the mattins, but as yet, no mass-bell— on a quadragesimal quarter-day and a rent-Monday too *and* washing-day, the wind like a scornpion and straight from Novgorod—a good drier!

But: the young sun
is in the fecund Ram, Gabriel already has said *Ave!* and stark wood lissoms. [1]

Coming up on a spring tide
with her Rotherhithe mate and her Limehouse skipper and a Sittingbourne bred pilot in her conning-house

his flag in the blow
in the morning.

Her main top-mast by the board, a stick of a jury for fore-mast, her mizzen-mast raked more nor natural and canted somewhat athwartships, sprung, woolded, but entire.

Her yards and sprits
and all her spars, all woolded; what you could see of her clewed-up main course were patched as a Welshman's quilt.

---

[1] See the Mass of St Gabriel, March 24; both Tract and Gospel contain Gabriel's salutation to Mary. The next day, March 25, is the Spring Equinox, the Feast of the Annunciation and Quarter-Day; it usually falls in Lent. The sun is in Aries from the second week of March to the same time in April.

We wont speak of her top-hamper nor the aspect of her dear,
gay garnishings[1]

                                                            but

sweet Christ's dear Tree!

                                    her cordage!!
how does it stand

                        to stay?
how does it run

                        to brace or lift or hale?[2]
can the wraith of a laniard extend the ghost of a shroud?

                            render or freshen, p'r'aps
but how take-up or belay

                        a hemp o' gossamer?
                        But, a cloth of buntin'
at her damaged main cap, another to pennon her jury

                                                            and
bended to the fretted halliers—not all that tattered and
bleached but what to gaudy yet her after-castle—

                                    her native ensign:
as proper to her as is the dog-rose to a' English beggar's hat,
abaft the weathered rags that served her for mizzen.

---

[1] 'Top-hamper' today is usually restricted in use to the light upper sails and
rigging, but historically it can mean any weight or encumbrance above deck.
In my text it is used of the built-up superstructures of medieval and later ships,
the decorations of which were termed 'garnishings'.

It is said that seamen and shipwrights both resisted the disuse of garnishings
which eighteenth-century utility demanded. Behind a natural dislike of change
and a proper love of decoration there were still deeper, if unconscious, reasons.
It is significant that the figure-head was still for so long retained; for in remote
antiquity the presiding genius of the vessel had her 'chapel' in the bows, and
again the stern had equally sacred associations as the place of command, helm
and ensign.

[2] Cf. the fixed system of stays and shrouds for staying the masts in position
called 'standing rigging', and that other and quite distinct gear of 'braces' for
bracing, 'lifts' for lifting and 'halliards' for haling (hale=haul) called 'running
rigging'.

There was no sign at all
of her bonadventure. [1]

She seemed but dressed
for Breaker's Yard
and, as she bring-to and were warped to her mooring
I saw water
coming from the *right* side, about midships; yet her list were
heavy to her lade-board [2]

and as I looked I saw:
she were hulled, SEVEN TIMES.

Yet fetching it
through all the fairs and fouls of:

the precessions
and heavenly conjunctions, eclipses, occultings and the
transits of the Wanderers

behaviours of water-spheres and atmospheres, as: incidence
of tide and peculiar pressures of the upper air.

Breezes
moderate to light, following zephyrs, light airs and dolphins
and mild birds of calm.

Backings, veerings

dead calm
becalms.

Shifts of unshaping mist.
Thicked shapeless hours by muffle of grey fog
grey hauls of wind
more wind
strong head-wind walls of wind
half-a-gale o' wind.

---

[1] Cf. *bonaventure* or *bonaventure-mizzen*, small mast positioned after the mizzen-mast in many late medieval ships.

[2] i.e. the left or larboard side, Middle Eng. *lade-borde*, the side from which the ship was ladened or cargoed up?

Thicks of rain.

      Gale!

      The weather 'gins to clear?

Then loom 'em red-tawnies!

       vancurrers of snow

and thunder-noons of yallery night

        and the dark night's

night-drench of white spindrift.

Scend by send of the sea.

Hove down of back-wash—

     into the wind

careened to leeward—

      of the wind.

    Green arcing darks

that thud inboard green-white, fore-castle[1] and after-castle

fretted and veronica'd of marrying falls of foam.

      (The conflux midships

were sea-boots high and well over.)

      All her sheer

the entire trembling keel-length of her vessel of burden

       silvered of

driven rain

       gilted of

bends of paly light

white as the Housel of spume.

     The tilted heavers

her oblation-stone

imménser hovers[2] dark-ápse her.

      Over where

unfathomed under her

    in the under-stills

---

[1] To be pronounced 'fore-castle', not 'foksl', in this instance.

[2] Pronounce ho-vers, noun formed on the verb to heave. Cf. Hopkins, *The Windhover*.

the washed-white margaron'd relics lie, where the pearl is,
as was the weather-eye of Ben Backstay

lux perpetua luceat ei

and upon all the precursors—as knowed their ropes—that
have gone before us under the regimen of the ship-star and
sleep the sleep with father Ulysses. [1]

. . . the full rant
of the Roarer and naughty tantrums of the lower heavens—
nor not all empty fury neither but signifying a jorum:

cataracted hail

flame along with it
sleet, sheet, fork, fire-balls

and water-spouts.

Captain, storm or hurricane, cap-tin?
you should know!

For certain this Barke

was Tempest-tost.

Shining exhalations
as appeared 'bout bate-time of storm-height.

FIVE on 'em

terrible lovely

starring the wide steer-board
and lade-board arms of the main yard, aflare far out-board of
her forward flare,[2] at the spumed bowsprit's lifted end, real
lofty beautiful at the mizzen-mast head

and

vapouring extra bright, from the after arm of the mizzen
yard, the wind-haled ensign-halliers with Helen's twin sign

sheening bluish

---

[1] Cf. Canon of the Mass, prayer, *Memento etiam Domine* '. . . who are gone
before us with the sign of faith and sleep in the sleep of peace'.

[2] The noun 'flare' is used by sailors of the upward bulge of a ship's sides or
the overhang of a ship's bows.

Forward is here to be pronounced 'forward' not 'for'ard'.

the wind-ratched red cloth of ensign

                          rejoicing them

for that she *cannot* be lost![1]

                   Vengeance of white great birds,
wraith-barques and phantom landfalls, undergirdings, jetson-
ings, neapings and groundings, fire 'tween-decks

                 fire in the orlop
                 fire in the hold.

                 Suasion by melody

of y'r genuine rock-sirens
twice as natural as the Mother of All Living, foam-white as a
Friday Venus, wetter nor Soo-zanna, clear gilt-tressed

---

[1] 'Shining exhalations that appere in tempestes', the fire of St Elmo or St
Clara or St Helen or St Nicolas, 'a vapor called by the Mariners a Corpo Zanto',
or, in Classical times, the fire of Castor and Pollux, the twin-brothers of Helen
of Troy; this phenomenon, under whatever patronage, has always been regarded
by seamen as beneficent, perhaps for the reason cited by William Dampier in
the seventeenth century '. . . the thunder and the rain abated and then we saw a
Corpus Sant at our main top-mast head. This sight rejoiced our men . . . for
the height of the storm is commonly over when a Corpus Sant is seen aloft'.
The colour of this electrical discharge is said to appear either bluish-white or
reddish. It was presumably with this phenomenon in mind that Macaulay
wrote:

                 Safe comes the ship to haven
                 Through billows and through gales
                 If once the Great Twin Brethren
                 Sit shining on the sails.

  And St Luke also, of gentile stock and tradition, could hardly have missed,
the significance of his own narrative when he wrote of the ship 'whose sign was
Castor and Pollux', that brought St Paul, after shipwreck and storm in another
vessel, safe to Caesar. Luke was writing a straight, ungarnished narrative of
actual events; had he been using those events symbolically and to subserve a
theme, he might have made the second vessel, that bore the sign of the Heavenly
Twins, suffer, but survive, the great storm. Cf. also *Macbeth* I, 3.

enough to hang a dozen Absolons[1]

                  and Lorks-a-mercy!

making a music to the tune of *Greensleeves* and for en-core in sung-out plain-spoke south-English, this prose:

                         With locks lovesome and long, with front and face fair to take between hands, with many mirths may we mingle, blow wind, blow us our sweetings[2]

set to fluvial fifths and fishy cadences of choirs fathoms under, but seeming of the Thirteenth Mode.[3]

                    'Twere the crux of the voyage and a near thing.

                            O, they was real bodily quicksand mammals alright, captain, though granted of a Faëry genus. . . .

May be, cap-tin, may be, but—and speaking under y'r professional correction—mirages dont commonly talk, nor fetter men by the sweets of descant, let alone toss from charm'd waves kist-posies of transaccidentated spindrift, under the form and several appearances of:

                        the primerole an'
                        the primerole an'
              the violet, the sweet Roman violet[4]

singular or entwined

          with the red rose and the lily-flower

---

    [1] See Chaucer, *Balade*
                  'Hyd, Absolon, thy gilte tresses clere . . .
                  Hyde ye your beautes Isoude and Eleyne.'
    [2] Cf. thirteenth-fourteenth century song, *Ichot a burde in boure bryht* (Ox. Bk. of Eng. V. No. 4).
    [3] The thirteenth, the Ionian Mode, is the mode to which the modern Major Scale corresponds. It was known in the middle-ages as the 'lascivious mode', that is, the sportive mode.
    [4] We are said to owe the violet to the Roman Occupation.

freshed of the cool water of
                              the well-spring[1]
exhaling distillations of the entire flora
                              and of WOMANKIND
to the man at the wheel.

No, captain, your mirage is but a mirage, this were nonesuch, ergo, this were no mirage but some other, even though fancy-bred and but apparently substantiate, still no mirage as commonly understood, or should my re-teller have told me untrue, then a ship-man's naughty lie: we may blast his sweet eyes but have still no mirage, neither on bow, beam nor quarter.

                              You see, Master,
I were not honoured of a' aurioled clerk to no purpose, nor *but* fleshly . . . and 'twere he that did name me when and as he would favour me, after the name[2] of her dower; and in the secret garth and inmost bailey of him, where such unlike conjoinings are, he did meddle me with his Bountiful Mother and with that *other*, that nourished him bodily: these *too* were England—if with differences.[3]

                              So that native-wise
and following the precepts of the spindle side and taught by horse-sense, yet primed of the nice embraces of sweet logic, I do affirm: All that is comprised under mermaid is no mirage.

---

[1] Cf. the Middle English song beginning 'Maiden in the mor lay' which K. Sisam described as a 'popular snatch' of the fourteenth century found scribbled on the fly-leaf of Bodley MS Rawlinson D.913.

[2] The name Angela is the name referred to because by a pious sentiment Anglia was named the 'Dower of Mary'—'*Non Angli sed angeli*'.

[3] Cf. the arms of Oriel College, 'England, engrailed for a difference'.

The short and the long being
that in this Matriarch's Isle we hold to water-maids:
this is the sound of the Findhorn stone![1]
That there be no water-maids you may tell to the marines as
manned the horse of Troy—but be warned in y'r temerity!

We *are* a water-maid
fetch us a looking-glass!
a comb of narwhal ivory, a trident
and a bower anchor—
and the Tower lion
nor twisk his lasher.
Here is our regnant hand:
this ring you see upon it were gave us long since by a'
ancient fisher; 'tis indulgenced till there be no more sea:
kiss it.
No, no, on y'r marrow-bones—though you hooked behe-
moth, you shall kneel!
This bollard here
where keels tie, come from all quarters of a boisterous world,
hand us to it to sit upon.
No Ægis?
Why then, for where our marbly shoulders socket the swan-
whites of our neck, and for our lilied front, knot and splice
the best soft-laid three-quarter inch halliard-hemp—and see
it shapes

---

[1] Joyce's washerwoman in *Anna Livia Plurabelle* says 'tell me the sound of the
Findhorn's name'; and the Foreword to the Ordnance Survey's *Map of Britain
in the Dark Ages*, North Sheet, referring to the symbol-stones of the Pictish
area, through which the river Findhorn runs, says: 'Several of these symbols,
such as the mirror, the comb and the boar, had a place in the later mythology of
the Celts in other regions . . . Is it not also possible that the mirror and comb
which are part of the equipment of that fabulous monster, the mermaid, may be
derived from the same cultural complex?'

for 't is to garnish paps
that nourish such as must strike soundings in the gannet's bath.[1]

If we furnish to the part
maybe we'll play it—as Saint Aristotle would 'a' said.
Our shift must drape so—no, a trifle off: but not indecorous!

No helm? no matter
we've mantling!

From over the chapman-booths of level
Southwark[2] does the stiffing breeze that freshes our Thames
play out our tresses—how this Maudlin gilt streamers a
tangled order

and sweet Loy!
how it do become us.

But La! late roses, red and white
with the earliest green acorn for our chaplet twined—you
little pretty one, you know our mind in head-pieces . . . and
these autumn fashions suit our complexion.

But who's gone to buy us
a bunch of blue ribbons?

capital!
now, let be at that

and let the Tilbury gulls
cry us Jack Neptune's latest espoused Jill and Last Thalas-
socrat.
Viols? Good—but see the mode's Dorian!

Dont eye *me*, captain
don't eye *me*, 'tis but a try-out and very much betimes:
For we live before her time.

---

[1] See *Anglo-Saxon Chronicle* under A.D. 973, '. . . over the rolling waters,
over the gannet's bath, . . . over the water's throng, over the whale's domain.'

[2] Cf. 'some of the war-host held booths in level Southwark'. *The Heimskringla.*
Section VIII, The Saga of Olaf the Saint.

. But to my tale
that I regaled my mason with—where were we?

Why yes:
Dartle and swift molestings of blackamoor Barbaries—as
hate IMAGE.

Cast-pieces bare cooled off,
harquebuses[1] fouled, arblests unstrung, jacks, gins and
ratches at sixes and sevens, matches damped, reserve powder
already using, ball very down, spring-stays and such like re-
placements not yet fitted, casualties scarce below, or by the
board, when what next? Siphoned Greek fire of the most
Christian Doge's dago latins amiral'd of a vandal of a baptised
Cypriot Jew from Damietta that was a camouflaged alcalif's
mameluke as by his algebras were a master of ballistics and
that by the sorceries of Apollyon had the wind at will
                                    it were the very Wicings!
for a full two hours or three.[2]
Unequal from the first contact and deteriorating rapid. The
mum and praying clerk as bended where was sighting of a'
all but crippled gun, straightens sudden and side-stepping the
recoil, uncommon actual, sings out:
            To prayers, all is won, all is won.
                                    To prayers.
And up went their powder-bin, aft of midships. Then echoes
the sergeant-gunner, broken on the deck:
            To prayers all is won
no matter where his commas come they've nowt bar
concedo to that one. You old God's arlot! well argued, that

---

[1] Pronounce hark-we-busses, with the initial aspirate strongly sounded.
[2] Cf. Song *Henry Martin*
            'Broadside on broadside and at it they went
            For fully two hours or three.'

makes clear, that *re*-distributes their middle[1] for 'em—now where's their premises? Ask of the strewed sea![2] But bless me you God's dumb hound: looks we'd best learn our trade anew, prove our back-sights by the Lombard and gloss the Scot before we know our rutters. By our own Nicomedy Barbara,[3] they felt the full Thisness[4] of that to each of the eight rhumbs of the four quadrants, either side the nording lily-flower or my name baint Wadman!

                          And other sharp exchanges
both sides the Pillars, as:
out come the Spagonies to dare and display in the wider *plazza* of the briny, and the Geeses with the looking-eye in both bows—goodish Sea-Peoples, both.[5] Then looms up the Lilies to gild the thirty-five leagues, and next, and now in the chops, the jack-o-lantern sea-marks of those caliban Corn-Welsh.

                          And then they sound
in the Channel of England, and

---

[1] Cf. how in syllogistic debate the term called the 'distributed middle' is the term shared by the major and minor premisses, and is the 'key-stone of the argument'.

[2] Cf. Felicia Hemans' *Casabianca*.

[3] St Barbara, virgin and martyr, executed in Nicomedia in Asia *c.* AD 230. She was imprisoned and martyred in a fort or tower which may account for her being the patroness of armourers, gunners, siege-engineers and such like.

[4] Cf. the term *haecceitas*, 'thisness', associated with John Duns the Scot and his principle of individuation, expressed in the well-known formula *Haecceitas est de se haec*, or, 'Thisness is wot makes this 'ere itself.'

[5] Cf. song, *Alfonso Spagony the Torreadore*.

The oculus in the ships of Mediterranean antiquity is still retained in some builds of Portuguese vessel and indeed in vestigial form in some English ones; for as recently as *c.* 1935, when staying at Miss Helen Sutherland's, I saw, in Embleton Bay, boats with markings suggestive of the oculus painted in their bows.

Frogs in the Sleeve apart, bear away for the Forelands. [1]
An' then, cap'n, for our English home-land beauties.

Without mention of the usuals
as: scurvies, cockroaches, melancholies, pent frenzies and
open mutinies.

The sawbones
that should mend 'em, a-voyaging in his Muslim book, the
priest, when not mum as a muffled oar, posing such as: Sirs,
consider nautics, is it in itself a good?

The Redriff mate
drove by this to venial retorts of rumps an' genitals, and
thence to such mortal blasphemies as might've brought down
the heavens and echoed in all the havens as there are from
Gothland to the capes of Trastamara.

The boatswain, from Milford,
for each circumstance finding antique comparison.

As though:
he were with them in the ships when they cast off at the rape
of Helen.

Were dozing
under his pent-house lid in the Downs roadstead, when,
Bang! bang!! there were Julius [2] stood-in for the South Foreland Light.

---

[1] See song, *Spanish Ladies*
v. 2 '. . . until we strike soundings in the Channel of Old England; from
Ushant to Scilly is thirty-five leagues' and v. 4 'and then bore away for the
South Foreland Light'.

[2] An English friend of mine living in Italy asked his Italian servant, who had
been to the cinema, what picture he had seen. The reply was, a naval battle
'in the old time', and a further query as to whose battle, evoked 'Bang, bang,
bang! perhaps Julius Caesar'. The film in question dealt with Lady Hamilton
and the hero of Trafalgar. I think it important to put this on record because it
provides a concrete modern example of the attitude of the Old Masters who
felt no anachronism in putting Herod or Darius or Joshua into medieval plate-
mail. The same unconsciousness of period was still operative in this man of the
Riviera di Levante in *c.* 1930.

Had made fast
a hove hawser for the first of the fathering tars of old mother
Troas to tie-up at the Downgate. [1]

Had conned their ship
for them as put Jonah by the board and were the man at the
steer-tree[2] in the Saving Barque that Noë was master of.

And not content
with ships of glass, voyaging islands and like old fablings

must aver
recent instances of islands that be males and females: [3] what
a carry on!

But, to put the cap on all:
that his Maddoxes, Owenses, Griffins and Company was a
type of sea-king and very lords of admorality as had held to a
course west by south till a new-found stony land were on
their starboard and south-south-westing in the offing of a
wooded shore fetched up in a vineyard, [4] with a whole cog-
load of mountain squires such as may be dabsters with a
coracle in a' estuary and as can handle the bulled oar of

---

[1] Called also the Dowgate, situated where the Walbrook fell into the
Thames (Cannon Street Station stands on the site), the earliest of all the ports
and quays of London, and in Roman times the principal if not the only one.
Troas used as the female personification of the Trojan thing, cf. Britannia, etc.

[2] Cf. *The Towneley Play of Noah*
'. . . tent the stere-tre and I shall asay the depnes of the see . . . '

[3] A phenomenon reported by Marco Polo.

[4] Cf. the eleventh-century Norse voyages to Stoneland, Woodland (Mark-
land) and Wineland (perhaps Newfoundland, Nova Scotia and New England
respectively) and cf. the legend of a Welsh twelfth-century transatlantic voyage.
Though this story of Madoc may be regarded as a legend given currency in
English in 1583, nevertheless it may reflect something of the Welsh contacts of
four hundred years previously with the Irish-Norse of Dublin and with the
Norse settlements in Wales itself, contacts which were particularly close between 1000 and 1150. Idea and myth no less than techniques of war and material
barter would be involved in these interchanges.

coasting currach, but seldom go on a' ocean-trip in a double-
ended sea-going nave, and as are, by a long journey, less
upsides with the modrcrn rig of a blue-water carrack than is
our Lord Mayor's pussy-cat and as like as not 'ld bend a'
ensign to a jack-staff

and then
vow by their devil's Davy Gatheren[1] that Trojan Brutus
learned them to fly 'em thus from halliards of papyrus in the
Third Age of the World.[2]

How so be that
he sweared by the Tree of Chester[3]
by a certain Jessy Mowers and by the owls, with many
darroes an' dammoes, Dukes and Jews and b' their god's
great athlete, Samson, and by Cassandra, as I take to be Welsh
for Delilah, though these two mortal women seem scarce
sorted, yet truly both was wheedlers.[4]
And by Our Lady of Penrice
the Welshman's most Blesséd Sibyl.[5]

---

[1] St Derfel Gadarn (cadarn=potent) famous throughout medieval Wales,
known in an English sixteenth-century rhyme as Davy Dervel Gatheren.

[2] Cf. the fourteenth-century Flores Historiarum, a pseudo-history of the world
from the Creation to AD 1326. The period covered is divided into six ages, the
third age being from 1921 BC to 1055 BC. The coming of Brutus to Britain is
placed in the twelfth century BC agreeing with the traditional date for the
Fall of Troy in 1184 BC.

[3] See

> 'There was a Welshman there . . .
> Now will I yield again . . .
> . . . . . . by the Rood of Chester.'

Langland, V. 579-586, Wells' trans.

[4] The Lady of the Pool of London is here giving her cockney version of: Iesu
Mawr, Great Jesus; y diawl, the devil; daro, colloquial for dammit; damnio,
damn; Duwcs, colloquial for Duw; Duw, God; Samson, St Samson of Dol; Cas
Andras, andras is colloquial for the deuce and cas means hateful.

[5] Bishop Latimer writing to Thomas Cromwell in 1538 says: 'I trust yr
Lordshype wyll bestow our grett sibyll to sum good purposse.' And again 'her
. . . of Walsyngham . . . of Ipswych . . . with ther other too systers of Dongaster
and Penryesse . . . They wold nott be all day in burnynge'.

By Tylows and Bynows unvouched of the Curia,[1] by fizt
Nut[2] the Welsh fairy, by the holy pillar of a Lacy or a
Lizzy[3] or some such, by the rigmaroled wonders of a most
phenomenal beast called the Troit[4] or such like, by a' elf-
sheen woman contrived of sweet posies,[5] by Arthur Duke of
the Britains, his three Gaynores[6] and his Pernels besides, by
Gildas the Wise and by Wild Merlin, by the marvel thorn of
Orcop and by the four fay-fetched flowers that be said to
blow where ever a' Olwen[7] walks in Wales

by the four Gospel true-tellers
and by the 'broidered tales

of Geoffrey, bishop of Asaph's
now deemed the most incontinent liar on record as the
Semprington sister did vouch me that could construe in

---

[1] St Teilo and St Beuno, sixth-century Welsh saints. Their cultus is locally,
not universally, observed.

[2] Edern son of Nudd (pronounce approximately nith, th as in 'thither'),
brother of the King of the Celtic Otherworld, appears in Romance literature as
a magician, Ider fitz Nut. In Old Welsh orthography Nudd would be spelt Nut
and as Nut he is known in French and English romance and is here to be pronounced 'nut'.

[3] Cf. Elise (el-issy) or Eliseg, a seventh-century leader in Powysland, where
his inscribed stone, called Eliseg's Pillar, still stands near Llangollen, unless
they've museum'd it.

[4] Twrch Trwyth, Porcus Troit, the object of the great hunt in the best of all
'task-setting' tales, *Culhwch and Olwen*.

[5] Blodeuedd, the woman made by enchantment out of oak-flower, meadow-
sweet and broom-flower in the tale of Math son of Mathonwy. Pronounce blod-
ei-eth, ei as in height, eth as in nether, accent on middle syllable.

[6] Perhaps owing to a Welsh fondness for triads there is a tradition that
Arthur had three successive queens, each called Gwenhwyfar. In Geoffrey of
Monmouth she is Guanhumara, a Roman patrician woman (how historically
right his instinct was, after all!); in Caxton, Guenever; in Malory's text,
Gwenyver(e); but in Old English, Gaynore.
It is a pity we lost Gaynore, for it rings as authentically English as 'salad-in',
'tully' or 'wipers', which cannot be said for Guenevere, now the received
English form.

[7] In the *Culhwch* tale four white trefoils spring up in Olwen's footsteps;
'therefore' says the narrative 'she was called Olwen' (*ol*, track, *wen*, white).

annals and in the modern findings of John Whethamstede a
great booker an' librarian

                a legist an' an Hertford man
this twice in his abbacy most able
a master of architects

             and a' impugner of fable.[1]

But Quo warrantoes?
    here's no surety

              for these learn'd be ever apt to
burn phoenixes and are like to bury the cat that has much
mousing in her yet, being but six times dead. I'ld as soon take
tale of Rose the dish-seller,[2] that meddles Maid Marian in
the Lay of Robin, with Luke's lay, *Then quoth Maria . . .*[3]
What odds, says Rosie, by Martha Betanny, these twain sort
as platter and pan and be as scarfed as keel and stem, in that
both lays ben 'gainst pretty sitters

             . . . which were close exegesis
and God's verity!
Howsoever, by all this and these this Welshook Milford bo's'n
sweared—as though it were matter greatly laden or of any
moment—by these he declared, so help him God,
how at this Welsh wave-faring

---

[1] John of Whethamstede in Hertfordshire, an administrator and builder and
twice abbot of St Albans, inaccurately known as the 'first opposer of Geoffrey
of Monmouth' and the first 'directly to oppugne the history of Brute'.

Whethamstede's many activities included (*c.* 1440) the writing of the
Granarium de Viris Illustribus in which Geoffrey's *Historia* is dismissed as totally
fictitious. But Newburgh and Cambrensis had said as much in Geoffrey's own
century without in any way affecting the continued popularity of the *Historia*
from its first publication in 1139 to the seventeenth century.

[2] Cf. '. . . Rose the dish-seller
   Godfry of Garlickhithe and Griffen the Welshman
   And an whole heap of upholsterers . . . '
Langland, V, 439-441. H. W. Wells' trans., 1935.

[3] Cf. Da cwaeth Maria: Min saule mersed drihten and min gast geblissode on
Gode minen haelende. Twelfth-Century English version of Luke I, 46.

when they stood to brim-ward
of Ongulsey Sound[1]
the out-mere to wander, untoward—
they wore their White Hound
for'ard.

Their quarterly gold and gules
four pard-cats counter-colour'd
at the main[2]
but aft
a red rampin' griffin.
Because, if you please
and 'now-opserve-you-close-nows-cabden'
Caesar from his stern-post
flew the same![3]
'T were *too* much.
Yet, you could not choose but hear, for as parson say of
Chrysostom, his tongue *could tell!*

---

[1] Some Northman gave the name Ongulseyjarsund to the Menai Strait, and
Ongulsey, later spelt Anglesey, to the island, which spelling gave colour to the
association with Angles; hence the false derivation, 'isle of the English'. An
error propagated by William of Malmesbury.

[2] The arms of Gruffydd, the father of the last Llywelyn, were: quarterly,
gold and gules, four leopards counter-coloured; on which account these arms
have in modern times been used to represent the principality of Wales.

[3] The dragon as an emblem in this island seems to derive from the *draco*,
the cognizance-flag of a Roman cohort, perhaps through the office of 'pen-
dragonship' in post-Roman times; rather as Bede says of the insignia of the
English Bretwaldaship that it was imitative of a Roman use.
Rome borrowed the *draco* from the Dacians in the second century AD and
later it became the Royal Standard of the Eastern Emperors, to be again
imitated in the West as a symbol of power. West-Saxon kings and others used it.
There seems no evidence of its use by the Welsh princes in the eleventh,
twelfth or thirteenth centuries, but there is documentary evidence that English
armies carried it *against* the Welsh in Plantagenet times. Glyndwr, however,
identified it with the Welsh cause and Henry Tudor utilized that tradition and
perpetuated it, so that the 'dragon of Cadwaladr', the *draconteion* of the Byzantine Roman Emperors, came to fly over Rugby fields and eisteddfod pavilions
in nineteenth- and twentieth-century Wales.

The cook scalded
the carpenter in irons—and
weevil in the biscuits.
Through all fouls and fairs natural.

As through all the filthy airs
what's work of transaccidentation, weft and warped of
glamour.
For he'll took on as second mate a Sandy from a port of call
north of the Bodotria.

Gup Scot!
they be more sotted than the Welshery
of grammarie.

Dont eye *me* captain
for I did but relate him as I were told, what I had of Ned
Mizzen, what he had of the late Ben Backstay's boozing
partner as was in her that trip.

Pieced in parts with
and descanted upon of certain matters told me on the water-
stairs by a dark foreigner of Pelasgian fathering, got upon a
Syro-Phoencian woman in the byes of Massilia that maze and
warren toward the mast-forest in the keel-haws of the Old
Port—whereabouts his tomb in that came quick from among
the dead. [1]

Signed on ordinary seaman
at Corbilo-on-Liger, [2] he that told me likewise of the peri-
ploughing, or the like, long long long ago, of a field of waters
he called the Erithrand [3]—though a long long long way from

---

[1] Marseilles is traditionally associated with the later life and death of Lazarus
and Mary Magdalene.

[2] At the mouth of the Loire, a port connected with the Cornish tin-trade of
pre-history and later. St Nazaire now occupies the site.

[3] See the account of the coastline from the Red Sea to the coast of India
known as *The Periplous of the Erythraean Sea*, written well on in the Christian
era, but attributed to Antiquity.

Crayford Ness![1] and reaching to the Malabarbers that our
Elfred sent to from Wantage, far far far back, that was the
brightest jewel of this land ever and a great layer of keels and
ought have his day in the calendar if any ever ought. Or else
the clerk of Bridgewater come lately from fishing in Tiber-
water, that sang to me *Come Hither Love*[2] in I-talian-cum-
Somerset, told to me false annals!

And further of them that,
once-upon-a-time, went by the south and came by the north,
in at the Narvesund via Spartel Head, homing over the
Middle Bight that leads to the Hill and navel of the world and
to the Two Lands, out from which, as clergymen sing, He
called his Son.[3]

That was hers
that laboured with him that laboured long for us at the winepress.[4]

---

[1] The Thames above and below Crayford Ness is called the Erith Rands.

[2] Cf. Chaucer, *Prologue*, 671-72,
> 'That streyt was comen from the court of Rome
> Ful lowde he sang Com hider love to me.'

[3] See *The Heimskringla*, The Ynglinga Saga, opening paragraph: 'It is said that
the earth's circle which the human race inhabits is torn across into many bights
so that great seas run into the land from the out-ocean. Thus it is known that a
great sea goes in at Narvesund and up to the land of Jerusalem.'

Cf. the gospel *Ex Aegypto vocavi filium meum*. Matt. II, 15.

Cf. the seventh-century-BC circumnavigation of Africa by the sailors of Necho
a king of Egypt; they sailed south from the Gulf of Suez to the Cape, home via
Gibraltar, to the Delta. They reported rightly that 'the sun was on their right
hand' for part of the voyage; a report that was incomprehensible to Herodotus,
who, two centuries later, wrote, 'I do not believe them'.

[4] Cf. 'The son of God suffered for us . . . like a lamb among wolves, lions
and dogs, labouring all that long time in the winepress of his blessed passion',
from *Langforde's Meditations in the Time of the Mass*, a fifteenth-century manual
for the laity.

When he came to town

> upon a' ass's pony:

At the lit board
and in the dark-hour[1] garden

> before the bishop's curia and
> within the Justiciar's mote-hall
> raised to the mock-purple

and

at the *column*, . . . cap-tin.

> On the ste'lyard[2] on the Hill

weighed against our man-geld

> between March and April

when bough begins to yield[3]

> and West-wood springs new.

Such was his counting-house

> whose queen was in her silent parlour[4]

on that same hill of dolour

> about the virid month of Averil

that the poet will call cruel.[3]

> Such was her bread and honey[4]

when with his darling Body (of her body)

> he won Tartary.[2]

Then was the droughts of March moisted to the root by that
shower that does all fruit engender—and do constitute what

---

[1] Accent on 'hour'.

[2] See the Good Friday processional hymn *Vexilla regis*, verse 5.
'Blessed tree on the branches of which hung the world's ransom. It became
the steelyard (*statera*) on which the body was weighed. And he bore off the
spoil of Tartarus.' (*Tulitque praedam tartari*.)

[3] Cf. anon. thirteen–fourteenth-century poem *Alisoun*
> 'Bytuene Mershe ant Averil
> When spray biginneth to spring.'
Cf. also T. S. Eliot, *Waste Land*, I, 1.

[4] Cf. Nursery Rhyme, *Sing a Song of Sixpence*, last verse.

they hallow an' chrism these clerks to minister that kings
and queens may eat thereof and all poor men besides.

                                      And other such prospectors
and others again and before again, such as chambered their
dead between the nebs and the nesses.[1]
                                 And before them
and before again, the precursors at the steer-trees
                                     many of them
in the old time before *them*.
                        These many, all long gone
                             dona eis requiem.
And the many yet to come that by some new-fangle shootin'
at the sun[2] shall check their rhumb-lines
                             dona eis requiem.
                        And those as after them
whose fathers shall relate to them of *these* old times before
them. Those as—by what new gear and a deal of dials, gins of
propulsion and all manner of contraptions, unguessed even

---

[1] The world-distribution of the megaliths is largely coastal; and tends in
Britain, at least in the Welsh coastal group, to be more on the lower slopes,
between, rather than on, the highest headlands.

Cf. the opinion that has seen in these monuments the dissemination of a cult
of the dead by mercantile companies prospecting for metal *c.* the second millennium BC.

[2] When in the fifteenth century the Portuguese first began to determine latitude by taking the altitude of the sun at midday, the new technique, called the
Regiment of the Sun, was received by sailors with reserve.

Prof E. G. R. Taylor writes, of English seamen, 'To see a man "shooting the
sun" (as it was already termed) with a cross-staff was an occasion for mockery.
"Have you strook it" he would cry, "Have you strook it".'

See *The Journal of the Institute of Navigation* for October 1948.

of a' admirable scab-shin Nominalist?—shall know the total compass of the thronging waters and assert regiment over the whale's entire domain.[1]

           And of these such, yet to come, a tidy many from the many hithes of this river, captain, by and large—some from this, here, very haw, captain . . .

dona eis requiem

sempiternam.

         And much beside have I learned as 'ld fill a book; of bazaar and mart, far parts and uses.

Much was I learned of these nautic gospellers I said and moreover I said I knowed some things out of Ovid's book and am well pleased with y'r company I said, but, I said, I'm no Sibyl, nor no Knower from Albi, nor female Daniel to figure out significations on walls, nor a ceromancer's mot, nor Taffy Merlin's mistress neither, I said.

         Though my ma was used to call m

My fine Lady of the Pool.[2]

---

[1] See the description of Drake's voyage of 1577-80 published in 1628 as *The World Encompassed*: 'touching ordnance and great guns, the late invention of a scabeshind friar among us in Europe' with reference to Bacon, known as *Doctor Mirabilis*, whose thirteenth-century researches make him a harbinger of methods and instruments without which sixteenth-century techniques and our own subsequent sea-power could not have been. In common opinion, if you were a Franciscan you were a Nominalist and certainly Bacon's preoccupations link him with Nominalism and with English empiricism. He appears to be nearer his namesake of 300 years later than to the saint from whom that namesake got his Christian name: though it's a long long way from Assisi to Verulam.

    Cf. the *A.S. Chronicle*, entry under AD 973. See note 1 to page 146 above.

[2] i.e. the Pool of London, and cf. Malory, IV, 1. '. . . than hit befelle that Merlyon fell in a dotage on the damesell . . . she was one of the damesels of the Lady of the Laake . . . And ever she made Merlion good chere tylle sche had lerned of hym all maner of thynges that sche desyred and he was assoted uppon hir, that he myght nat be from hir.'

    Cf. also the familiar theme of ladies of pools, fountains and rivers in tales deriving from Welsh sources.

[159]

May she rest in Arthur's bosom
I said, and signed me against the General Resurrection.
After what narrating I were something put for wind.

But to what he answered nothing
but seemed shook down to more comfortable matters
which served well

for now was full dusk and
the replete moon, wore, I thought, a wry and homely smile.

But, captain, from that
most august eve I saw him no more.
They come and they go, captain.

But by what lode's regimen
or Jacob's staff 'ld y'r bearings be took in those waters?

—these freestone masons
has queer runes, captain.

But he were as cunning
a tow-haired Jute as ever plumbed an' levelled dark I-tie-wise
—and they be fairish artiers, captain, from Maidstone way[1]
as can pier a stream-bed with any pontiff or gauge from base
to apex to satisfy a Rhodópis—entasis and all.[2]

At the Fisher with the ring, 'pon Cornhill[3]

---

[1] Owing, it is believed, to previous Frankish contacts, the Jutes of Kent are known to have had a higher material culture than the other Teutonic settlers in Britain, and there are reasons for thinking that a tradition of civilization was less disrupted in Kent than in other parts of the island.

[2] Cf. Tennyson, *The Princess*, 'The Rhodope that built the pyramid'.

Just as in ancient Greece, columns were made fuller at the middle to prevent any appearance of concavity so, in Egypt, were the pyramid-surfaces made subtly convex for the same reason; and in the middle-ages, spires were sometimes given this same entasis and again for the same reason.

[3] In London usage the second syllable in 'Cornhill' takes the stress accent.

St Peter-upon-Cornhill was, in twelfth-century popular tradition, the oldest Christian church in London and was believed to have been the seat of the first metropolitans and to have been founded by 'Lucius son of King Cole'.

A stone commemorating the legendary foundation by Lucius stood in the

which was the first hill-site in Brutes Albion
to be made other for the lifted Sign.

Where 'Wellin Fletcher, Wildgoose Lane,
b' ste'lyard merchants wharf, reckoned to see Old King Cole
him solid self standing next Lucy's stone at service time, in a
candidate's vesture; about when they fetch the big fair-
garnished percher, lighted to the fonted water, after the
fourfold and blest dividing of it, to conjoin with, make quick
and fertile, that innocent creature; just 'fore they start up
the Kirry lees'ns of the Whit Sat'd'y, cap'n. [1]

Which fletcher's skimble-skamble tale makes a'
honest body feel all ov'rish an' druidical: May the Sign fend
me from his Welshery!

At 'Hallows [2]

by the shameful tree
where the molls pray the Hanged Man and his
Dolorosy Queen.
At so many bliss'd sites
what body knows to whom they all hallow'd be? [3]

---

church in the sixteenth century and here druids were believed to have received
baptism. What this curious tangle of legend reflects we do not know, but it is
to be noted that the site is very near the accepted site of the basilica and chief
forum of Roman London, on the higher ground east of the valley of the Walbrook. There is other high ground west of that stream and these twin acclivities
have continued to determine the focal points: the Guildhall, the Old Bailey
and St Paul's on the one hand and the Leadenhall, Lloyds and the Royal Exchange
on the other. It is probable that this site has very ancient sacred associations,
Christian and pre-Christian Roman and, conceivably, pre-Roman.

[1] The ritual of blessing the font at Easter is repeated at Whitsun; the Paschal
candle extinguished on Ascension Day is specially re-lit to be again immersed in
the newly blessed water in the 'womb of this divine font' as the liturgy says.

[2] All Hallows, Barking-by-the-Tower.

[3] '. . . there were many more churches there than they might wot to what
man they were hallowed' from a description of London in Snorri Sturlason's
twelfth-century *Heimskringla*, 'The Saga of Olaf the Saint'.

At ad Vincula[1]

wrong side the blooded moat

at fair-triforium'd John[2]

in the darks of the White Turris

(that's where they keep the chopper bright, captain

and no candle

to light you to bed).[3]

At every rounded apse-end

where the flamens plead his death who is Best and Greatest[4]

on the mind-days[5]

when we mark with the white stone.

In each blithe *aedes*

as gables a bell-rope.[6]

At the crutched-signed brothers, where the Three Mothers

—in their wide laps the orchard-spoil, sit,

crofted under.[7]

At the One Uncreate and Singular Three, East Gate, where

the three created fays do play

---

[1] St Peter ad Vincula, within the outer baily of the Tower.

[2] The chapel of St John in the White Tower.

[3] Cf. how in a Commonwealth document, the Tower axe, then required at Whitehall, is referred to as the 'bright axe'.

[4] Cf. the pagan dedications *Iovi Optimo Maximo*, which can with even more significance be applied to the God addressed by Launcelot as, 'Fayre (swete) Fadir Jesu Cryste'. Malory, XVII, 15. 'swete' not in Winchester MS, but in Caxton. And also the London tradition mentioned by Jocelin of Furness (twelfth century) of pagan *flamines* becoming Christian *episcopi*.

[5] The day of anniversary on which a *memento* was made in the Mass, for some benefactor or any person deceased. E.g. Stow's *Survey*, 1598, 'Robert Chichely grocer, mayor 1422, appointed that on his mind day a competent dinner should be ordained for two thousand four hundred poor men'.

[6] Cf. Dunbar, *In Honour of the City of London*, 'Blith be thy chirches, wele sownyng be thy bellis'.

[7] Cf. the carved stone fragment of the three seated female figures holding fruit and flowers, known to represent the *Deae Matres*, whose cult was popular in Britain as in Gaul and Germany, found under the site of the church of the Crutched Friars in Hart Street, Aldgate.

under

worked extra antique in the creature of stone

under.[1]

At each adytum over

where under the fathering figures rest that do keep us all.

So it's fabled

in Taffy's historias and gests of Brut the Conditor—

romans[2] o' Belins, 'Wallons an' Wortipors[3]

agéd viriles[4] buried under

that from Lud's clay have ward of us that be his townies—

and certain THIS BOROUGH WERE NEVER FORCED,

cap-tin!!

And making to bear

bean-stalks, cherry-gardens, tended 'lotments, conserva-

tories and stews of fish, pent fowl, moo-cows and all manner

o' living stock, such as, like us women, be quickened of

kind: so God will.

Strong binders also

to make our loam the surer stereobate for so great a weight

of bonded courses,

so it is said.

---

[1] Cf. the Roman sculptured stone believed to represent three nymphs found
on the site of the priory of the Holy Trinity, Aldgate.

[2] romans, accent on second syllable, but said as an English word, not as a
French one.

[3] Apart from the head of Brân the Blessed buried under the White Tower
and chief protector of London and of the Island, in Welsh tradition, there were
other hidden guardians and strength-givers: Brut the founder, Lud, Beli,
Cadwallon, and Vortimer (Vortiporius) the 'good' son of the 'bad' Vortigern.
By means of Anglo-Norman chroniclers and writers of *romans* and *bruts*, vestiges
of this deposit became a permanent part of English lore, whether folk or liter-
ary; to be felt in later centuries as a kind of ground-swell and sometimes as a
present wind influencing such a deep-draughted ship of burden as the *Shake-
speare* or the high-superstructured *Milton*.

[4] Pronounce to rhyme with 'tiles'.

[163]

Though there's a deal of subsidence hereabouts even so:
                    gravels, marls, alluviums
here all's alluvial, cap'n, and as unstable as these old annals
that do gravel us all. For, captain:
                    even immolated kings
be scarce a match for the deep fluvial doings of the mother.
                    But leastways
best let sleepers lie
                    and these slumberers
was great captains, cap'n:
tyrannoi come in keels from Old Troy
                    requiescant.
For, these fabliaux[1] say, of one other such quondam king
rexque futurus.[2]

                    And you never know, captain
you never know, not with what you might call metaphysical
certainty, captain: our phenomenology is but limited,
captain.

                    So of these let's say requiescant
till the Sejunction Day!
For should these stir, then would our Engle-raum in this
Brut's Albion be like to come to some confusion!
                    You never know, captain:
What's under works up.

                    I will not say it shall be so
but, captain, rather I would say:
                    You never know!

---

[1] X in fabliaux to be sounded.

[2] Cf. Yet som men say in many partys of Inglonde that Kynge Arthur ys
nat dede but had by the wyll of oure Lorde Jesu into another place, and men
say that he shall com agayne. . . . Yet I woll nat say that hit shall be so . . .
men say that there ys wrytten uppon the tumbe thys: *Hic iacet Arthurus Rex
quondam Rexque futurus.* Malory, XXI, 7.

In all the white chapels

in Lud's town of megara[1]
when we put up rejoicing candles bright
when we pay latria

to the Saving Wood.[2]

About the turn of the year, captain, when he sings out loud
and clear from his proper: *in ligno quoque vinceretur*[3]

twisting his cock's egg tongue round

the Vulgar *lingua* like any Trojan licentious of divinity.

And him but got within Billingsgate,

in Puddin' Lane, on her that calls hot herring-pies—whose
smile's as sweet as her marjoram: what's got her to church
door three times without mention of her pre-history.

And *at* the turn, captain, *pridie*

the thirteenth and all, we carry out Chloris as dead as a nail.[4]

---

[1] Cf. the meaning of the place-name Megara, 'the temples'.

[2] Things as signs occasion the kind and degree of honour due to what they signify. The cross, considered purely as a sign, happens to be the specific and unique sign of God the Son the Redeemer of the World, and, as such, occasions divine honour, latria. To offer latria to the cross, crucifix or relic of the cross, *qua* sacred object, image or relic, would be idolatrous. But to offer anything less than latria to the cross, *qua* sign, would be to offer something less than latria to what is signified (namely the Redeemer) which would be insufficient, or rather, an impossibility. For which reason, using the inexact language of everyday speech, we say we pay latria 'to the Wood', because the word 'wood' or 'tree' here signifies the stauros, and the stauros is the singular sign of our Redemption. Cf. page 180 below.

[3] See the proper Preface for masses of the Passion, used on the Feast of the Exaltation of the Cross, '. . . and he that overcame by the tree *on the tree might also be overcome* . . .'

This feast, called in England Crouchmass or Holy Cross Day, when the wood of the cross is venerated, falls on September 14; so that it has relationship with the end of summer, September 12, and with the Ides of Autumn, the 13th, and with the Ember Days of September which themselves take their position in the liturgical cycle from the seasonal change in the cycle of nature; cf. the approximate concurrence of the other Ember periods with the beginnings of winter, spring and summer.

[4] See preceding note.

'T will soon be on us, cap'n
it'll soon be here.
Flora's late come soon gone
                    in Cronos-*meer*.
You'd best weigh
            you'd best be off, skipper
you're wrong side the Pillars
for this tide o' the year
                    you in y'r carvel-built—an' look at
her fished spars![1]
Lorks! you ancient man
                you'd best weigh!
I'ld make a whale of a mere-maid, captain, had I scales to
m' belly.

                            Come buy!
Come buy, good for between the sheets, good for all ails o'
the head an' nerves.
B' the bell'd clout o' Martin, you'll owe me only five
farthin'.
Buy m' livid flower
                            there's good souls!
There ducks!
                an' a' extree sweet bunch from the Sud Ridge[2]

---

[1] Carvel-built in contrast to clinker-built ships, and composite yards or other spars, in contrast to spars made from a single length of timber, characterized Mediterranean in contrast to northern shipping. To lash lengths of wood together to form a single spar is called 'fishing'.

[2] Surrey lavender, from the Mitcham district, was, and is still, famous on the London market; see note 1 to page 125 above.

for a pretty boatswain's boy. There's a poor curly—and
fairish for a Wog—not a' afreet but a' elfin!

                      Plucked with his jack bucket from
the Punic foreshore b' a bollocky great Bocco procurer, or
I weren't christed Elen Monica in Papey Juxta Muram. 'V'a
mind to sign him Austin Gregorians in Thames-water, an'
ransom him with m'own woman's body.[1]

                                Captain!
Spare him the rope's end, captain, for love of the Mistress of
Lodemanage whose storm-quelling Son made crost Belin's
drink[2] as though he walked the solid causey over m' dancin'
Lady Lea;[3] Him as the Senate and People of Rome, for fear
of the synagogue and people o' Moses, had roved quick to
the Blesséd Yard afore Eight Bells on the Friday

                                or, captain
though I wish no harm to y'r lawful occasions

---

[1] See the parish, long extinct, of St Augustine Papey or St Augustine-in-the-Wall, Aldgate Ward; the dedication was to Augustine of Hippo; Papey, possibly 'of Pavia', where were relics of that saint. Cf. also the conversation of the latter with the child on the seashore and also Botticelli's painting of that scene. Cf., further, the story of the Angle slave-children and St Gregory, Pope, who sent the *other* Augustine to England.
    Pronounce 'Juxta' as an English word.

[2] In an early Welsh *englyn* the sea is called 'Beli's liquor'. This Celtic sky-god had water-associations, hence his legendary eponymous connection, by way of Cuno-Belin (Cymbeline) with Billingsgate fish-market and water-gate. Lud, the other supposedly eponymous figure, is the same god as Nudd or Nodens and is also associated with rivers and estuaries. London is both Urbs and Ostia and, however much etymology may invalidate the old opinion that connected such London names as Ludgate and Billingsgate with figures from a Celtic past, that tradition nevertheless shows a sure grasp of the mythological requirements *vis-à-vis* the site and in that sense has a permanent validity.

[3] From Aldgate the Roman road to Colchester was built across the marshy flats of the Lea River.
    Cf. the song, *London Bridge is broken down*
                   Dance my lady Lea

[167]

by Gogmagog!

and the thirty-two fornicating
daughters of the Island o' Britain,[1] may the Loathly Worm
have you, before you've so much as made the Nore on a
favourable tide! I know your fund of amusements and you
macaroni admirals is worse nor Trelleborg sea-kings.

Who'll have

m' living flower?
Who'll buy my sweet lavender?

*　　*　　*

[1] The Guildhall images known as Gog and Magog, destroyed by fire in 1666
and in 1940, were known until the seventeenth century as Goemagot and his
Trojan victor Corenius. Goemagot was the last survivor of the giants of Albion
begotten by incubi on the 'emperor Diocletian's thirty-two wicked daughters'
that had come to Britain. Thus, it appears, is the Trojan legend fused with
memories of an historic proscription of the Christian Church in our collective
London myth. It will be recalled that our proto-martyr St Alban suffered under
the Diocletian persecution early in the fourth century AD. As with the individual
psyche, collective myth cares nothing for discrepancies of time or circumstance.

VI
KEEL, RAM, STAUROS

Did he hear them bawling a Frigg-day's ichthyophagous feast
at the Belling Gate?[1]

(Is that why
they back-cant on Parnassus?)[2]

Did he walk the water-lanes of the city from east of Bridge
Within, by Dowgate and Vintry to Farringdon Without.
Walking the nine river-fronting divisions of the city[3]
of cities all, *per se*
and flower of towns[4]
did he hear them say
when will you pay me?
(or had they not yet grown rich?)
when might that be?
when might that be??
I do not know!
I do not know!!
I do not know what time is at
or whether before or after
was it when—
but when *is* when?
All that we do know is
that from before long ago he
sailed our *Mori Marusam.*

---

[1] In contradiction to the supposed traditional connection of Billingsgate with
either a Celtic god, Belin, or a Celtic king, Cunobelin, or to the accepted
derivation from an English personal name, Billing, it is suggested by others that
the word derives from an Old English verb, *bellan*, to cry out.

[2] Cf. Boileau, *L'Art Poetique;* Canto I, 83-4 translation adapted by John
Dryden, 1683. 'All except trivial points grew out of date Parnassus spoke the
cant of Billingsgate.'

[3] Nine of the twenty-six wards of London have river-frontage.

[4] Cf. Dunbar.

'London thou art of townes *A per se*
. . . art flour of Cities all.'

Wot sort o' Jute-land lingo's that
or is it Goidel for
>Mortuum Mare?
or did old Gaius Pliny
>get his Pytheas wrong
or had the travelled diarist
>gravelled his philology
in Cronos-*meer?*[1]
Has he been on the spree

>with Nodens
>in Lydney woods[2]

Was ever he ashore with
>the shining *mamau* of Usk?[3]
Don't say he's a mate of Manawydan's:[4]
Keltoi on land are twisters enough!
He's some rare chinas

>beyond the Pillars.
He looks a bit of a clencher-build
>himself.

---

[1] Pliny, following a writer whose authority was the travel-diarist Pytheas, says that *Morimarusam* was the name used by the Cimbri of Jutland for that part of the North Sea in which our island is situated. The Cimbri were a Teutonic people whereas the word *Morimarusam* appears to be Celtic and equates with Welsh and Irish for Dead Sea and Pliny says that it did mean *mortuum mare* and that it extended to the Sea of Cronos, the name used by the Classical writers for the unexplored northern waters. This note is based on some remarks of the late Sir John Rhŷs, much of whose philology is, I understand, now regarded as ill-founded.

[2] Nodens, Nudd, in Irish Nuada, in English tradition Lud, a war-god but associated with the sea, with ports and estuaries. His great shrine was at Lydney on the Severn.

[3] *mamau*, *au* as ei in height, accent on first syllable, mothers.
In some parts of Wales the fairies are called 'the mothers' and this is thought to derive from the cult of the *Deae Matres*. See note 7 to page 162 above.

[4] Manawydan, man-now-wid-an, accent on third syllable. The Irish form is Manannan, the Celtic sea-diety. He is a magician in the medieval tales.

His bends are of thick stuff!
He's drained it again and again they brim it.
'T's a marvel he knows for'ard
nor after.
It's wonder the owners stand for it
                                    consid'rin' the
lading so precious
up to the highest board.[1]
Gunwales under last bon voyage.[2]

                                        Contingent risk:

the're all in the swim.

Listen: when it's adieu to y'r[3]
                        Miletus ladies
when it's farewell to you
                        Lady of Thebes
when we founder
            when we embrace the sea-stript dead
wher'l they be?
away with the coverage
                        on a proper siren's cruise.
That's how they work it
                in Pluto's Thalassocracies.
Where 'ld be their bleedin' miracle
that is Graecia
                but for us ones
as cargoes-up
                the thousand ships?
Caulk it, m' anarchs
                he's fixed you
with his ichthyoid eye.

---

[1] Cf. carol, 'There comes a galley laden up to the highest board'.
[2] Pronounce as though English, not as in French.
[3] Pronounce as 'ard-yer t'yer'. My Greek seamen speak cockney.

Aye, the old ichthys!

Who else should they choose
to handle the bitch
(and what a crew!)
if not the cod's-eye man?
the bacchic pelasgian
disciplinarian.

But watch his
disciplina
beyond the gangways aft
abaft
the trembling tree.

Down
far under him
the central *arbor*
the quivering elm on which our salvation sways.
Baum, baulk
ridging the straked, dark
inverted vaults of her.

Base-line
(for the drawers of elevations and sections in the
water-side offices and for the mast and block makers also
the determining factor):

Yardstick, prime measure
(for those concerned with admeasurement
volume, draught, load-draught

[173]

berthage, sight-draught, brokerage
exchange and mart—and, policy:
                    Kegged butter or, cradled *tormenta*?)
Spine
        for her barrelling ribs
tallest and chose beam
                    to take her beams.
Prone for us
                buffetted, barnacled
tholing the sea-shock
                    for us.
Three-nailed the strakes to you
                garboard, bends and upwards
free-board and capping and thole.
All wood else hangs on you:
clinkered with lands or flushed with seams.
                    Raked or bluffed.

Planked or
        boarded and above
or floored, from bilge to bilge.
Carlings or athwart¹ her
horizontaled or an-end
                tabernacled and stepped
or stanchioned and 'tween decks.
                    Stayed or free.
Transom or knighthead.
Bolted, out in the channels or
battened in, under the king-plank.
Hawse-holed or lathed elegant for an after baluster
                cogginged, tenoned, spiked
plugged or roved
                    or lashed.

---

¹ Pronounce athort.

And all things other
          fast or easied:
bellied full
          or brailed and furled.
For a poet's gale or for a navigator's:
in a hard blow or before a zephyr.
Belayed or paid or gone
          for a headfast or for a clew-line.
Before and standing, for a stay, a-straddle for a ratlin'd
shroud or running and braced after.
Grommetted, moused; parcelled, served.
Two-stranded marline
          or straight-cored
heart-of-hemp hawser
               altus[1] and hoist
at the cathead or bowered to the fundus.

          And the thewed bodies
the true-hearted men so beautiful
          between perpendiculars
and over-all.
          Timber of foundation
chosen as stoutest and topping them
forechosen and ringed
          in the dark arbour-lands.

To be set up?
          pole for the garlands?
gibbet

---

[1] *altus* is here to be pronounced as awl-tus.

for the dented *spolia*?

gibbet at Laverna's cruxed-way

for dolorous queans to mourn an Adonis *ad vincula*?[1]

Or horizontal'd?

ceremonially dressed

the whole complement paraded

awaiting the venerable man

his pallid boy with his book and bucket.

His homily's text:

'*Satur fu fere Mars*

—leap the *limes*!

He can gloss text and context

for a park of ordnance.[2]

Asperged?

the better to wear-down the proud?

High-platformed, for the Borer

brought to bear from a city-taker

or medium-light

and swung

for a *falx*-arm, to glean

the standing crennel-course.

---

[1] See the goddess Laverna, patroness of malefactors, and cf. *Beggar's Opera*, Air III, Cold and Raw.

'A Rope so charming a Zone is!

The Youth in his Cart hath the Air of a Lord

And we cry, There dies an Adonis!'

[2] Cf. The Hymn of the Arval Brethren:

Satur fu fere Mars: limen sali

which is said to mean:

'Be satiated fierce Mars, leap the threshold' but which, it is thought, may have originally run:

'Be thou sower, sower Mars, sow the soil.'

So that the priest come to bless the siege-engines, in substituting 'frontier' for 'threshold' is only underlining a metamorphosis already suffered by Mars the agriculture god.

Ossifraga for his personnel?
       then lammergeyer for his
last draft of under-aged. [1]
Or, preponderant
             very great (to date)
             composite, experimental.
Of selected boles, *orneus*, assembled and tied with iron or of
tall beams, coniferous, bolted.

  Thirty paces and a bit from butt to business end—well
above the maximum last show-done—eleven an' a half hands
thick where she takes her war-head.
                   Show-piece
for the immaculate *tribuni*, temporarily attached, battering-
train.
Storm-goat, rodded in the Æsir's yard[2]
for the blond, acting, Under-*optio*, beleaguer-group.
For the layer, from Londinium:
              A bit o' alright.

Given pet agnomina?
            the Mauler, the Leaper
Marmor's other flail, Bellona's left
            the Thunderer's *right* dook.
Half a mo Hector, Bumping Hecate, Long Doris
                  Lysistrata No. 2.[3]

---

  [1] The largest type of assault-towers were called 'city-takers'; the various
weapons were operated from platforms at different levels, the *terebra* to bore
into the wall and the 'wall-sickle' (*falx muralis*) to engage the loosened masonry
of the upper courses and as it were reap them down together with the personnel
manning the crennels.
  [2] Cf. *Sturmbock*, the German name for the Roman military *aries*, and cf. Asgard,
the Olympus of the Northern peoples.
  [3] Cf. the meaning of Lysistrata's name, 'Dissolver of Armies'.

Off the secret-list?

                 maximum impact
                 penetrative power
                 bias, rebound
                    effect of 'X' releases
on propulsion-gear, deficiencies
serious defects
listed in detail for the coded files
summarized for circulation to affected departments
metamorphosed for general release?[1]

Or vertical'd?
dendron

           for a torch-goddess?

ashera

           to vermilion and incise?

Erect?

           for the wheat-waves to be high?
           for the sea-wattles to be full?
for the byres to be warm with breath, for the watering by
precedence[2] to be clamorous?

                        for the lover's lass?

---

[1] Ammianus Marcellinus in describing various siege engines says 'Now we come to the ram. A tall pine or a mountain-ash is selected.' In the foregoing passage I envisage a developing armament. As with the other assault engines, the weight and mechanization of the ram increased. From being a simple length of timber carried by a number of men it appears to have become a contrivance swung from heavy supporting beams.

[2] Those who have watered cattle will remember that those animals tend to observe some sort of order of precedence at the drinking-trough. They will not easily allow 'Daisy' to drink before 'Cowslip'.

For the dedicated men in skirts to cense
before, behind, above, below
                              on the glad invention morning?
Are the faithful given authenticated fragments?
Do these fastidious
                    exorbitantly perfected
                              red, and as

roses-on-a-stalk
reach to salute you
                    along with the shapeless and dowdy pious
and the pious donors, and, brow-bright Pietas herself
just where, just now
                    with what's left of lips
the swaithed incurable that crept unseen
                    left his unseen mark?
Do these patina, do they enhance
do they quite wear-down
                              your adzed beauties
slowly, century on centuries
with fond
          or efficacious, salutes?
Knowing the changing *fasti*?
Sometimes palled? sometimes
stripped by the sacristans?
Diurnally, and for the Nocturns
Polyhymnia comes and goes?
at any hour the maimed king
                              pays a call?
Twice a century—perhaps
                    for nine days or so

Demos
with crisis in his unnumbered eyes
                    importunes counter-wonders?

[179]

Day by day
        the sustaining lauds
of the few?
Occasionally?
          Phryne
regularly?
          Lais
          for a quick decade?
Sometimes the flambeaus
        with the flora mingled?
mostly a penny flame or two?
often the votive bunch
          plucked out of school?
Always lifted up?
        seen of the polloi?
reckoned worthy of latria?[1]
loved of the polis?
         evident hope of it?
         Agios Stauros
stans?[2]

         Recumbent for us
the dark of her bilges
          for fouled canopy
the reek of her for an odour of sweetness.
Sluiced with the seep of us
knowing the dregs of us.
Hidden wood
        tree that tabernacles
the standing trees.

---

[1] See note 2 to page 165 above.
[2] 'Holy Cross standing?'

Lignum for the life of us
      holy keel.

Ship's master:
    before him, in the waist and before it
          the darling men.
Cheerily, cheerily
     with land to leeward
known-land, known-shore, home-shore
home-light.
       Cheerly, cheerly men
'gin to work the ropes.
And she bears up for it
      riding her turning shadow.
The incurving *aphlaston* lanterns high above him
behind him
     the plank-built walls converge
to apse his leaning nave.
To his left elbow
      the helmsman
is quite immobile now
      by whose stanced feet
coiled on the drying hemp-coil
     with one eye open.
the still ship's cat
     tillers, just perceptibly
her tip of tail.
He inclines himself out-board
      and to her-ward. [1]

---

[1] i.e. toward the figure of Athene above the harbour to starboard. See p. 96 above.

The old padrone

        the ancient staggerer
        the vine-juice skipper.

What little's left

        in the heel of his calix
asperging the free-board

        to mingle the dead of the wake.
Pious, eld, bright-eyed

      marinus.

Diocesan of us.

        In the deeps of the drink
his precious dregs

        laid up to the gods.
Libation darks her sea.
He would berth us

        to schedule.

*   *   *

VII

MABINOG'S LITURGY

1 The country between the Middle Rhine and the Upper Danube is the European fatherland of the Celts; it was from South-West Germany that the Celtic Iron-Age culture sprang.

Viridomar (the leader of the combined Celtic armies defeated by 'the great Marcellus' at Clastidium in 223 BC) called himself 'the son of the Rhine'.

2 The sculpture known as the Dying Gaul is in fact a copy in stone of one of the bronzes from the groups of figures of defeated Celts which decorated the acropolis at Pergamon in the second century BC.

3 Although the word *caliga* denotes, for us now, an essentially Roman thing, the field-boot of the Roman Army, both word and thing are said to derive from a Celtic source, together with certain other articles of military use including the *sagum*, and, it seems, the word *gladius* itself.

4 Celts were serving as mercenaries in Ptolemaic Egypt and four such at Abydos in 185 BC left a scratched memorial of themselves on the walls of a chapel of Horus: 'Of the Galatians, we Thoas, Callistratos, Acannon and Apollonios came here and caught a fox.' That four privates off duty in a strange land should chase a jackal and call it a fox and record the event fits perfectly with all we know of serving soldiers of today. Cf. H. Hubert, *The Celts*.

The inscription is in Greek and the names are Greek, but we know from St Jerome that even five centuries later the Galatians of Asia Minor, the descendants of the various groups of mercenaries, still retained their Celtic dialects, though long since Greek in culture.

I use the Welsh word *llan* because it comes direct from Old Celtic *landa* which in turn is cognate with the German key-word *Land* and so equally with our own integral English word 'land' and our delectable English word 'lawn'.

5 That is, a hundred and twenty years or so. From the time when the Teutonic Cimbri of Jutland appeared on the north Italian frontier (103 BC) the bogey-men for the Roman council-chambers, and we may be sure, for the Roman nurseries, were no longer Celts, but for the first time in history, Teutons.

6 Cf. the anonymous early Latin lullaby,
> '*Lalla, lalla, lalla*
> *i aut dormi aut* lacta'.

7 Amminius, the brother of Caratacus and son of 'Cymbeline', but of the pro-Roman faction. During the century between Caesar's invasion and the Claudian occupation, Belgic Colchester (Camulodunum) had been open to the cultural and economic influences of the Roman world and the successors of Cunobelin were divided in policy. I use the names 'Caratacus' and 'Amminius' as symbols only of the two reactions to that state of things when the full weight of a materially powerful and advanced civilization is brought to bear upon peoples of a far earlier culture-phase.

8 I have supposed the Incarnation to have been in 5 BC or 4 BC that is AUC 749 or 750, and have followed the tradition that our Lord was in his thirty-third or thirty-fourth year at the time of his Passion.

Two centuries
                    since Rhine-progeny[1]
became dying Galatae
                    in Pergamon bronze[2]
and four caliga'd[3] other ranks
                              torque-wearers
                              off parade
started a fox
                    on Nile bank.

By their *Hausnamen* no longer called, their *nomina*
already Anatolian:
not now of *Wald* or *llan*
                    but, of the *polis*.[4]
Four generations[5] of fretful charges since first our nurse-
maids warned us:
    That's *Teutones*
                    come to fetch you!
    brats that neither sleep nor suck
                    bogle Cimbri gobble up.[6]

Upwards of two hundred and fifty years
                    since West-*raum* seekers
brought La Tène to Thames-side.
Caratacus a growing son.
Belgic romanophils
                    already half toga'd
in Camulodunum
                    but keep, as yet, their trousers on.
Amminius yet our creature?[7]

In the seven hundred and eighty-third year[8] of the Urbs, the
Mother, fourteen years since the recovery of the Eagles,

[185]

forty-two come the 7th before the Ides of July since they decreed

Peace in Our Time[1]

the whole world expectant of war.

TiberiusClaudiusNeroCaesar

voted the tribune's powers for the

first time twenty-five years since; his fourth term consul nine years gone.

West-rites *defensor*
conservator of provinces
        in the fifteenth of his pontificate.
Father of his country, world-*soter*
    for four years now on his palmy beach
but to speak once yet
        as if from the City to the World.[2]
Lucius Ælius Sejanus

senior officer, combined command

(Castra Praetoria). Chief law-officer (criminal jurisdiction) outside the City.
Co-ordinator of groupings:

civil, military
security, secret.

Holder of the key portfolios

---

[1] Cf. the senatorial decree of July 9, 13 BC, authorizing the building of the Altar of Peace on the Field of Mars at Rome to commemorate the conclusion of war in the West and to symbolize the Augustan pacification of the World. There have been Temples of Peace built in our time also.

[2] The policy of Tiberius was to support the official religion of Rome as against the non-Italic and non-Western cults which were gaining ascendancy. In AD 26 he began his retirement on Capri where he died in AD 37, but in AD 31-2 there was the swift action that liquidated Sejanus and the staged trip up the Tiber as far as the walls of the city, to the applause of the people. He did not come ashore.

place-giver and power-channel.
Venerated in image on the legionary *signa*[1]
        his weather-eye on the Diaspora.
Joint-Consul
Prime Minister
cosmocrat
          in his apex year.
But one more yet before they have him, before Tiber, by
way of the Mamertine, has his broken body.
Lucius Ælius Lamia
         nominate legate of Syria
still not posted.
Under the fifth procurator
        of Judaea
in the third or fourth
        severe
        April
of the ten, sharp
        Aprils of his office.[2]
On Ariel mountain[3]
        on Flail-floor Hill
(here the articulated instrument of wood and here the
bruised flesh for the wheat-offering.)[4]

In the early month
        with late frost

---

[1] The effigy of the minister, Sejanus, was worshipped among the standards of
the legions, as though he were himself emperor.

[2] Pilate was governor of Judaea for the exceptionally long period of ten years
(AD 27-37). It was the opinion of Tiberius that change of governor meant only
fresh bleeding of a province by the new nominee.

[3] Cf. 'Woe to Ariel, to Ariel, the city where David dwelt.' Is. XXIX, 1.
(A.V.)

[4] Cf. 'and the threshing instruments for wood and the wheat for the meat
offering'. I Chron. XXI. And cf. the instrument joinered for 'the sweet load'.

                    for sharp spines
that's all the balm he'll get
                    of Gilead brake
this late-lambing year:[1]
(Already they have put wood into his bread)[2]
But eighteen days to the Maying.[3]
                    They say it's Tuesday's child
is chose
this year's Mab o' the Green
                    mundi Domina
or was she Monday's
                    total beauty
Stabat by the Blossom'd Stem?[4]

Thirty-four years
          (now that the March Lucina's past)[5]
thirty-four years and twenty-one days
since that germinal March
and terminal day

                    (no drought that year)

---

[1] See note 1 to page 52 above.

[2] Cf. Maundy Thursday, at *Tenebrae*, 3rd Nocturn, responsary following Lesson VII *Venite mittamus lignum, etc.*

'Come let us put wood into his bread and root him out of the land of the living.'

[3] The 14th of April: eighteen days before the Kalends of May.

[4] Cf. the Nursery Rhyme:
            'Monday's child is fair of face
            Tuesday's child is full of grace'
and the Tract in the Seven Sorrows Mass:
Stabat sancta Maria caeli regina et mundi domina juxta crucem . . . 'Stood holy Mary, queen of heaven and mistress of the world, next the cross', and the Gradual in the Mass of the Immaculate Conception: *Tota pulchra es Maria* . . .

[5] Juno under the title of *Lucina*, light-bringer, the goddess of birth, was honoured at the beginning of each month, but the month of March was hers especially.

since his Leda
                    said to his messenger
                              (his bright *talaria* on)
fiat mihi. [1]
Thirty-three, back last early fall
since the hamadryad
                    leaning from Pomona's wall
showed her ripe cherries
was first to keep the rubric's word:
                              hic genuflectitur. [2]

Within the thirty-fourth year
                    from the Stille-night
since wolf-watcher's rollick
                    and blithe introit
in Pales brighted yard
since Hob, to his butty, Goodfellow
                    cried: *Transeamus.* [3]
Thirty-three Janus-nights gone [4]
since the night
                    of the Showing
                    to great Estates
since three dukes *venerunt:*
halted Arya-van
                    at Star-halt.

---

[1] See the Mass of the Annunciation, March 25; terminating words of the Gospel: . . . *fiat mihi secundum verbum tuum*, 'be it unto me according to thy word'.

[2] Cf. the carol '*Joseph was a-walking*' in which the cherry-tree genuflects to honour the unborn Son and for the pregnant Mother to eat; and the familiar rubric 'Here all kneel'.

[3] See the gospel for the Second Mass of Christmas Day: ' . . . *Transeamus usque Bethlehem*', Luke II, 15. 'Let's go over to Bethlehem'.

[4] As with Juno, so with Janus: the first day of each month was sacred to him; but his main feast was annually on the first of his own month of January.

Our van

       where *we* come in:

not our advanced details now, but us and all our baggage.[1]

In this year

       at the shrill, cruel, lent of it

the young sun well past his Ram's half-course, runs toward the Bull.

The virid shoots precarious and separate as yet on the fronding wood.

       You can see: One, two . . .

I can see three . . .

       Five!

       there

there on that old baulk

       they've polled

for Summer Calend's tree.[2]

Aunt Chloris!

       d' sawn-off timbers blossom

          this year?

You should know.

       Can mortised stakes bud?

Flora! surely you know??

---

[1] See the Gospel for the Epiphany, January 6:
'*Magi ab oriente venerunt, etc,*' Matt. II, 1. 'Magi from the East came.'
And cf. 'and they were Gentiles and in this Gentiles we, so come we in.' Sermon XIV of the Nativity series of Lancelot Andrewes.

[2] On the analogy of a terminology connecting us with Antiquity and still used in one part of this island. In Wales May Day is still called *Calanmai*, the Calends of May, the Summer Calends. The Winter Calends, *Calangaeaf*, fall in November and these two days were the two pivots of the Celtic year, as are similar dates among other pastoral peoples.

You who decked *die Blumendame* and our Blodeuedd formed. [1]

           Lovely Flora

how variant you are.

               You can tendril and galloon

chose queens, *im Rosenhage* [2]

had you no hand in

          this arbour

               too?

But surely?

        No?

        then where's that Sibyl?

Well, run and fetch Calypso [3]

            out for to see

she 'ill be only moping

              over an old tale

              in the half-light

              on the back balcony

that gives towards the sea.

She's sibylline enough

        she too knows dendrite beauties.

           And little Persephone

those Five she'ld *love* to pluck.

---

[1] Blodeuedd, blod-ei-eth, ei as in height, eth as in nether, accent on middle syllable. The maiden contrived of meadow sweet, oak flower and broom flower in the tale of Math son of Mathonwy in the *Mabinogion*. From *blodau*, flowers.

[2] Cf. the appellation *Maria im Rosenhag* used of pictures of our Lady in a floral setting—in the rose-arbour.

[3] In his book *Cumaean Gates* Mr Jackson Knight, on page 30, writes, 'Calypso is very much like a sibyl' and on page 32 he develops this idea. In his *Vergil's Troy*, page 93, the same author refers to the possible connection between Calypso ('she that covers') and the name Helen and the association of that name with moon-goddess and tree-goddess. It will be recalled that Zeus compelled Calypso to let her lover Ulysses sail home to Ithaca and leave her on the sea-shore of Ogygia after she had enjoyed him for eight years.

They're the freshest
                    ever you saw.
And old Nestor
                    fetch him
bad blind old man
he'll like not know
                    another spring.
. . . then let's prop his lids
                    p'r'aps he'll see a bit:
he lives to collate phenomena.

Martha! stop that endless meddling!
and dont tie Argos up
                    or, he'll bark
the place down.
He's a nose for what springs new
from hoar stem
                    and ancient holm.
Let him come gently.
See! he would reach to lick
                    the trickling blossoms
by the ancient stone.[1]

---

[1] Cf. the carol known as *The Corpus Christi Carol*.
                    ' . . . there standeth a stone
                    Corpus Christi wreten thereon'
                                        (verse 6, MS. circa 1400)
                    '. . . there lieth a hound
                    which is licking the blood as it
                    daily runs down.'
                                        (verse 6, Derbyshire, recorded in 1908)
            'which ever grows blossoms since Christ was born.'
                                        (verse 7, North Staffs, recorded in 1862)
And cf. *Odyssey*, Bk. XVII, 291-292.
'A dog lying there raised up his head and ears
(This was) Argos (the dog) of . . . Odysseus.'
Cf. page 242 below.

In the first month
in the week of metamorphosis
the fifth day past
at about the sixth hour after
          the dusk of it
toward the ebb-time
      in the median silences
         for a second time
again in middle night-course
         he girds himself.[1]
Within doors, attended
      with lamps lighted.
No hill-*pastores* lauding[2]
      for Burning Babe
      for Shepherd-Bearer.[3]
      Nor now far-*duces* star-night
nor swaddlings now:
his *praetexta* is long since cast.
      Is it the tinctured *picta*
he puts on?
Yes, and the flowered *palmata*
      by anticipation:
this *is* 'his own raiment'.[4]

---

[1] Cf. the Introit for the Sunday within the Octave of Christmas, *Dum medium silentium*. 'When all things were in quiet silence and the night was in the midst of her course thy almighty Word, O Lord, came down from heaven . . .

'The Lord is clothed with strength and has girded himself.' Wisdom XVII and Ps. XCII (Vulgate) Ps. XCIII (A.V.)

[2] Cf. Christmas carol, *Quem pastores laudavere*.

[3] Cf. Southwell's *Burning Babe* and Paul's (?) 'that great shepherd of the sheep'.

[4] The *praetexta*, as worn by children, the *toga picta*, dyed red with gold stars, and the *tunica palmata*, purple embroidered with palm-leaves, worn at triumphs. See Matt. XXVII, 31, ' . . . they took the robe off from him and put his own raiment on him', and Isaias LXIII, 1-2, 'Who is this that cometh from Edom with dyed garments from Bosrah, this that is glorious in his apparel, travelling in the greatness of his strength. . . . wherefore art thou red in thine apparel'. (A.V.)

Not *Lalla, lalla, lalla* [1]

      not rockings now
nor clovered breath for the health of him as under the
straw'd crucks that baldachin'd in star-lit town where he
was born, the maid's fair cave his dwelling.

           Brow of Helen!
hide your spot that draws the West.
No! nor cast eyes here of green or devastating grey
           are any good at all.
Had she been on Ida mountains
to whose lap would have fallen y'r golden ball, if not to hers
that laps the unicorn? [2]

               And you!
She has your hunter's moon as well.
Vanabride! y'r cats come to her call. [3]
Whose but hers, the Lady of Heaven's hen? [4] and, as Dürer
knew, the butterfly is proper to her himation. [5]

---

[1] See note 6 to page 185 above.

[2] It will be remembered that Helen's beauty was enhanced by the mole in her forehead and Aphrodite's by the cast in her eye. There was also the blemish in one eye of the British Venus, Emma Hamilton, which took 'nothing from her beauty'. And further that it was in the Ida range of mountains in Asia Minor that Aphrodite's offer was accepted above those of Hera or Athena and that perfection of form won the apple and not riches nor even success in battle. Paris' values were not at all bad. Further again, that only virgins can tame unicorns and that in some allegories the unicorn means our Lord.

[3] Vanabride is Freyja. See note 2 to page 59 above.

[4] By the European peoples, Greeks, Romans, Celts and Teutons, the wren, the smallest of birds, has been called the 'king of birds'. Frazer cites the Scottish folk-rhyme:

      'Malaisons, malaisons, mair than ten,
      That harry the Ladye of Heaven's hen.'

[5] See Dürer's painting the 'Virgin with the Irises'. The madonna is in a red dress with a purple cloak upon the paler purple lining of which a butterfly has alighted. From the Doughty House Collection, now in the National Gallery.

Look to y'r title, Day-star o' the Harbour![1]

        . . . in all her parts

tota pulchra

more lovely than our own Gwenhwyfar[2]

        when to the men of this Island

she looked at her best[3]

        at mid-night

three nights after the solstice-night, the sun in the Goat, in
the second moon after Calangaeaf;[4] with the carried lights
that are ordinary to her before her and the many *plygain*-
lights[5] special to this night about her; the *yntred*[6] sung, the
synaxis done, at the beginning of The Offering proper,[7]
when they light the offertory-light that burns solitary on the
epistle side; standing within the screen (for she was the wife

---

[1] See pages 94 and 96 above.

[2] Gwenhwyfar, gwen-hooy-varr, accent on middle syllable.

[3] See *The Lady of the Fountain* '. . . more lovely than Gwenhwyfar the wife of
Arthur, when she has appeared loveliest at the Offering, on the day of the
Nativity or at the feast of Easter'. Guest's translation.

[4] Calangaeaf, cal-an-gae-av, ae as ah+eh said quickly as a monosyllable.
Winter-calends, November 1.

[5] *Plygain*, plug-ein, ei as in height, dawn. This name is given to a Christmas observance when people assembled in the parish churches, lights being
carried and carols sung. The hour varied, but in the eighteenth century it
appears to have been at dawn. The many lights characterized this observance
and it is the lights which are remembered. A church in Flintshire was burnt in
1532 and according to a nineteenth-century writer the fire was caused by the
Plygain lights, 'in imitation of the High Mass, a custom particular to Wales'. As
1532 antedates the suppression of the Mass in Wales, this statement is very
ambiguous, but it shows that the Plygain was *regarded* as a surrogate for something lost.

[6] *Yntred*, Introit, un-tred, accent on first syllable. The *synaxis* (meeting) is
that part of the Mass preceding the offertory prayer.

[7] Strictly speaking the Mass essentially begins at the offertory prayer. In
Welsh the Mass is called *Yr Offeren*, The Offering.

of the Bear of the Island)[1] and toward the lighted board; in cloth of Grass of Troy and spun Iberian asbestos,[2] and under these ornate wefts the fine-abb'd Eblana flax, maid-worked (as bleached as will be her cere-cloth of thirty-fold when they shall intone for her . . . *pro anima famulae tuae*[3]) and under again the defeasible and defected image of him who alone imagined and ornated us, made fast of flesh her favours, braced bright, sternal and vertibral, to the graced bones bound.

If her gilt, unbound
(for she was consort of a *regulus*) and falling to below her sacral bone, was pale as standing North-Humber barley-corn, here, held back in the lunula of Doleucothi[4] gold, it was

---

[1] Cf. the thirteenth-century gloss on a MS of Nennius, which reads: 'Artur, translated into Latin, means *ursus horribilis*'. There is also the exceedingly obscure passage in Gildas where he calls some ruler Ursus, the Bear. There seems every reason for rejecting the suggestion that Gildas here refers to Arthur; but it may be noted that in Old Celtic the word for bear was *artos*, modern Welsh, *arth*.

[2] Cf. the stuff called *gwellt troia*, 'Grass of Troy' mentioned by medieval Welsh poets, for example in *c.* 1450 'Grass of Troy like a maiden's hair, the Son's countenance in delicate embroidery', and in the same poem, *ystinos*, asbestos, is mentioned, 'A stone we know is spun come from great India to Gwent'. And in 1346 'Stockings of thin brilliantly-white asbestos; and this is what asbestos is—a precious brilliantly-white stone which is found in Farthest Spain, which can be spun'. And in 1520 'Bi-coloured sheen of Greek embroideries fit for nobles of the Round Table . . . a work of fire'. See F. G. Payne, *Guide to the Collection of Samplers and Embroideries*, Nat. Mus. of Wales, Cardiff, 1939.

[3] Cf. the requiem mass for a woman deceased, ' . . . on behalf of the soul of thy handmaid, N. etc.' and see Malory, Bk. XXI, on the obsequies of Guenever, 'And than she was wrapped in cered clothe of Raynes from the toppe to the too in thirtyfolde.'

[4] Doleucothi (dol-ei-coth-ee, ei as in height, accent on third syllable) in Carmarthenshire, the only place in all Britain where gold was continuously mined in the Romano-British epoch. Many gold ornaments have also been discovered on the site.

paler than under-stalks of barley, held in the sickle's lunula.
So that the pale gilt where it was by nature palest, together
with the pale river-gold where it most received the pallid
candle-sheen, rimmed the crescent whiteness where it was
whitest.

      Or, was there already silver to the gilt?
For if the judgmatic smokes of autumn seemed remote,
John's Fires were lit and dead, and, as for gathering knots of
may—why not talk of maidenheads?
Within this arc, as near, as far off, as singular, as the whitest
of the Seven Wanderers, of exorbitant smoothness, yet
puckered a little, because of the extreme altitude of her
station, for she was the spouse of the Director of Toil, [1] and,
because of the toil within,

               her temples gleamed
among the carried lights hard-contoured as Luna's rim,
when in our latitudes in winter time, she at her third phase,
casts her shadow so short that the out-patrol moves with
confidence, so near the zenith she journeys. [2]

               If as Selenê in highness
so in influence, then as Helenê too: [3] by her lunations the
neapings and floodings, because of her the stress and drag.

---

[1] Cf. 'At Llongborth saw I of Arthur's brave men hewing with steel (Men
of the) emperor, director of toil', from a fragment in Early Welsh translated
by the late John Rhŷs.

[2] Those who have had occasion to move about in Forward Areas recall that
it is possible, if disconcerting, to do so in bright full moonlight, provided that
the moon is high in the sky.

[3] Selenê and Helenê are so accented because the proper English forms,
Selene and Helen, do not preserve the phonetic similarity of the two names, a
similarity said to disclose a far more important mythological correspondence
between Helen and the moon-goddess. See Jackson Knight, *Virgil's Troy*.

   . . . for she was the king our uncle's wedlocked
wife and he our father and we his sister's son.[1]

And from where over-gown and under-gown and *linea*
draped the clavicled torus of it, her neck-shaft of full entasis,
as though of Parian that never ages, still as a megalith, and as
numinous:

                  yet, as limber to turn
as the poised neck at the forest-fence
                     between find and view
too quick, even for the eyes of the gillies of Arthur, but seen
of the forest-ancraman (he had but one eye)
                    between decade and *Gloria*.

                    Downward from this terminal,
down from the wide shoulders (for she was a daughter of the

---

[1] Owing to the success of the later Launcelot-Guenevere theme as a romance
motif, the earlier, more basic and more political theme in the 'moste pyteuous
tale of the morte Arthure saunz gwerdon' has been somewhat over-shadowed.
I mean the destiny of Medraut (Mordred) 'For ys nat kynge Arthur youre
uncle and no farther but youre modirs brothir and uppon hir he hymselffe
begate you uppon his owne syster? Therefore how may ye wed youre owne
fadirs wyff?' Malory, XXI, 1.

It seems not improbable that this Medraut theme contains elements of genuine
historicity. It represents the tradition of a power-struggle in Britain between
the *dux*, Artorius, and a group of his *equites*, during the forty years or so of peace
that followed the halt of the Anglo-Saxon barbarians at the siege of Badon Hill.
It fits in with what is known to the historians of the sub-Roman world. The
intrigue involving the wife of Artorius in the traditional story is historically
possible and such intrigue certainly fits in with the censures of Gildas against
the British leaders a generation later.

tyrannoi of Britain and these Arya were *cawraidd*)[1] down
over the high-laced buskins (these the *Notitia*[2] permitted)
to where the supple Andalusian buck-skin, freighted from
Córdoba, cased her insteps (for all the transmarine nego-
tiators, prospectors, promoters, company-floaters and *mercatores* laded and carried for her) covering all but the lower
eyelet-rings and the thong-tags and other furnishings of polar
ivory

to obtain which

who but Manawydan himself, on the whale-path, but four
and half degrees of latitude without the arctic parallel, two
hundred and twenty nautical miles south-east by south of
Islont[3] with Thor's Fairy-Haven[4] Isles looming on his starboard beam about six Gaulish leagues, alone and by himself—
except for his *môr-forwyn*-mates[5]—running free with the
wind on the starboard side, carried away and handsomely,
the rare dexter tooth of the living bull narwhal that bluff-
nosed the southwester nose-ender with spiralled ivories
lancing the bright spume scud.

The cruising old *wicing!*

---

[1] In Welsh tradition one of Arthur's Gueneveres (there were three) was the
daughter of Gogyrfan Gawr; the epithet *cawr* means 'giant', but it may also
mean 'tyrant' in the sense used of Œdipus. *Cawraidd* is the adjectival form of
cawr (*-aidd* as eith in either).

[2] The *Notitia Dignitatum Imperii Romani* was an official compendium dealing
with a variety of subjects from the dispositions of the defences of Britain to the
number of lights carried before members of the imperial family. The Occidental
section that has survived was issued early in the fifth century. While having
this directory and book of etiquette in mind I am not citing a specific item.

[3] Islont, iss-lont, accent on first syllable, called also Ynys-yr-Ia, Island of
Snow, Iceland.

[4] The Faeroe group.

[5] *môrforwyn*, sea-maiden, morr-vorr-win, accent on the penultimate syllable.
As has already been noted, Manawydan, man-now-ud-an, was a sea-god and
perhaps an agriculture-god, who appears in the tales as a Welsh ruler with
magical powers.

This he averred he achieved on his ocean-trip to the Thing-
Ness in Gynt-land,¹ his *hiraeth*² upon him, some fifteen days
out from his *dinas* in Cemeis in Demetia³

          (where he latins his oghams).

Plotting his course by the North Drift route that streams
him warm to Hordaland

          to Noroway o'er his faem

over the gurly brim in his mere-hengest

          (he's stepped the Yggdrasil for mast!)

To the Horder's moot in Norvegia

          over the darkening mere-flood

on a Gwener-Frigdaeg noon.⁴

          (To add a bit *more*

to his old *mabinogion*?⁵

          Will he Latin that *too*

to get some Passion into his Infancy?

---

¹ Thing-Ness, from thing (assembly) and ness (promontory). It has been
suggested that there is a connection between this compound and the Welsh
word for city, *dinas*, din-ass, accent on first syllable. Gynt, 'g' hard, from
gentes, the Scandinavian peoples.

² *hiraeth*, heer-aeth, ae as ah+eh, the Welsh word for yearning or longing,
is also found in place-names as in the Hiraethog hills in Denbighshire, and there
is the theory that connects the word with a site-name envisaged in a Welsh-
Scandinavian complex. In his book *Mabinogi Cymru* (1930) Mr Timothy Lewis
gives a map showing a suggested cosmology of the world of the old tales and on
it 'Hireth' is identified with Hordaland, now the district of South Bergenhus in
Norway.

³ Demetia or Dyfed is South-West Wales.

Cemeis, kem-ice, accent on first syllable.

This ancient division of northern Pembrokeshire is said to be the home of
much that went to the formation of the oldest legendary deposits.

⁴ Cf. the ballade, *Sir Patrick Spens*,

'To Noroway o'er the faem' and 'And gurly grew the sea'.

Cf. *brim* and *mere-flod*, for sea in O.E. and *mere-hengest*, sea-horse (mare) for
ship. Friday or Frig's Day is Dydd Gwener in Welsh; Gwener from *Veneris*.

⁵ *Mabinogion*, mab-in-og-yon, accent on third syllable. The singular is
mabinogi (mab-in-og-ee) the repertoire of a *mabinog* (accent on second syllable)
a tyro bard; and meaning also a tale of infancy as in the tale called *Mabinogi Iesu
Crist*. The root is *mab*, son, as in Maponus (Mabon) a Celtic god sometimes
equated with Apollo.

By the Mabon!! he will
when he runes the Croglith,[1]
in all the white bangors[2]
of the islands of the sea
where there is salt
on the Stone within the *pared*.)[3]

Or, was he a liar?
Did he and his back-room team
contrive this gleaming spoil from fungus by Virgil's arts in
Merlin's Maridunum?[4] Or, did he barter 'em, ready-made-
up, in Bristol? He might have done either, the old conjurer!

Downward then
obscuring all, over all the numinous whole, over all the knit
parts other than the column of her neck and the span-broad
forehead and whatever strong enchantment lay between forehead and chin:

---

[1] Croglith, 'Lesson of the Cross'; crog-lith, accent on first syllable. In Wales
Good Friday is called Dydd Gwener y Groglith, *crog*, cross, plus *llith*, from
lectio.

[2] The word *bangor* means the top row of rods in a wattle fence. As the Celtic
religious communities were enclosed in such fences the word appears to become
applied in some cases to such enclosures. Cf. the place-names Bangor Iscoed,
'the *bangor* below the wood', and Bangor Fawr, 'the great *bangor*'.

[3] *pared*, *a* as in parry, accent on first syllable. A dividing wall (from *parietem*),
here meant of a chancel-screen.

[4] Cf. The *Mabinogion*, where Manawydan practises the craft of cobbler and
where Gwydion uses fungi as his medium which by transaccidentation he
causes to have the appearance of richly harnessed horses. In Wales, as elsewhere,
Virgil was associated with magic and so with alchemy, but in Wales today
chemistry is still 'the art of Virgil' (*fferylliaeth*) and any chemist, Boots' Cash,
is 'an agent of Virgil' (*fferyllydd*).
Maridunum was the Roman name for Carmarthen, which is an anglicism for
Caer-Fyrddin, which means Merlin's fort.

We are not concerned with portrait
but it can be inferred that of her eyes, one was blemish'd.

Over other than all this, and excepting only these terminal
forms, mantling the whole leaning column (which was the
live base for these) covering for the most part the handsome,
well-shaped Dalmatian tunic of gold stuff inter-threaded
green (the stitched-on dark laticlaves kermes-dipt) that had
beneath it the convenient, well-fitting, glossy under-gown
of shining fire-stone, that hid all but entirely the long,
bleached, well-adjusted, comfortable vest that sheathed
immediately the breathing marble.[1]

      Habiting all and over all
from top to toe (almost)
ample and enfolding

        in many various folds
with the many lights

        playing variously on the folds
her wide *lacerna*[2].

---

[1] Cf., with regard to these clothes, the interesting examples, given by T. C.
Lethbridge, of the probable influence of the Classical forms on the Celtic and
Teutonic peoples, even those outside the Roman world, and as late as the
Norse-Irish wars. (See *Merlin's Island*, 144-145.)

[2] *Lacerna, paenula, planeta, phelonion, amphibalum, casula*, in Welsh *casul*,
in English chasuble, by whatever name, this rational, probably Ionian,
garment became increasingly fashionable in the Roman world from the third
century and was still worn in the seventh century; to be subsequently retained
by the conservatism of the Church, so that clergy still wear it in 1950, but now
only if they are priests and only at Mass and only if they are celebrants of the
Mass. When these, who alone are now privileged to wear it, kiss it and put it on,
perhaps they sometimes remember that had not Roman, sub-Roman and post-
Roman persons of various sorts and their wives and daughters worn it as a
customary top-coat, they would not now be wearing it as the specific sign
of those who represent rational man and who offer a rational sacrifice under
the forms of bread and wine. About 400 the chasuble was compulsory for
senators, and in a contemporary painting (cited by Duchesne), Gregory the
Great (540-604), his father *and his mother* are each wearing it.

(As near the sacred *murex* a length o' cloth
as ever come out of a Silchester madder-vat!)

And moreover
patterned the colour of gorse-buds in forms as *apis*-like as
may be.
(Ischyros and all his Basils! what will they say of that at Caer
Gustennin?) [1]

Edged and lined throughout
with dappled vairs of marten and pale kinds of wild-cat:

It's cold in West-chancels.
So, wholly super-pellissed of British wild-woods, the chryselephantine column (native the warm blood in the blue
veins that vein the hidden marbles, the lifted abacus of native
gold) leaned, and toward the Stone.

And on and over the stone
the spread board-cloths and on this three-fold linen the
central rectangle of finest linen and on the spread-out part
of this linen the up-standing calix that the drawn-over
laundered folds drape white. [2]

And before the palled cup
the open dish and on the shallow dish and in the wide bowl
of the stemmed cup

the three waiting *munera*:
Of Ceres

from the reserve-*granaria*

---

[1] Cf. the purple chasuble embroidered with golden bees, worn at Byzan-
tium as the exclusive prerogative of the imperial house. Caer Gustennin, keirr,
ei as in height, gis-tén-nin; Constantinople.

[2] Three linen cloths, one over the other, are used to dress a Christian altar.
During the action of the Mass a further piece of linen is spread centrally and
on this the chalice and paten are placed. Cf. the older method of covering the
chalice with part of this linen cloth (corporal), a use still followed by the
Carthusians at Cowfold and I suppose by them elsewhere.

(for Elbe-men
blacken with red fire the east wheat-belt, and nothing through
from Loidis,[1] and elsewhere the situation is obscure and
Nials gathering hostages[2] gather also the white sign, and then
on top of all and everywhere the blackening by grey rain for
three successive years of rotten harvest).
Of Liber
                    perhaps from over the Sleeve
made confluent with the lucid gift
our naiads never fail to bring
                    parthenogenic from the rock
quick by high valleys, or
                    meandering slow and
by the wide, loamed ways, by sallowed way
                    sign the whole anatomy of Britain
with his valid sign
                    (out to where the nereids
bring in the shoal-gift: also Him, in sign).
No wonder
                the proud column
                    leaned
to such a board
even before the Magian handling and the Apollinian word[3]

---

[1] Cf. Loidis Regio or Elmete, the British district in the West Riding. In
my text the name 'Loidis' must be taken symbolically of any pocket of resistance
in times of confused and shifting frontiers; I am not implying that 'Ilkley moor'
was in fact grain-producing.

[2] Cf. Nial of the Nine Hostages (whose last raid in the Severn area may
possibly have been the occasion of the carrying off the future St Patrick), and
such-like Irish raiders who, during the fourth, fifth and sixth centuries, were
to the west of Britain what Saxons were to the east and Picts to the north.

[3] The ref. here is to Spengler's terms, 'Magian culture' and 'Apollinian
culture'. The manual act of consecration in the Mass is of the former culture,
while the words of consecration are generally in a language of the latter.

that shall make of the waiting creatures, in the vessels on the board-cloths over the Stone, his body who said, DO THIS for my Anamnesis. [1]

By whom also this column was.

He whose fore-type said, in the Two Lands

I AM BARLEY. [2]

It was fortunate for the innate *boneddigion* [3] of Britain that when at the prayer *Qui pridie* [4] she was bound as they to raise her face, she as they, faced the one way, or else when the lifted Signa shone they had mistaken the object of their Latria; to add to the taint of the Diocese of Britain an impulse more eccentric from the New Mandate than is the innate bias of the heresiarchs of Britain.

In the middle silences of this night's course the blackthorn

---

[1] Anamnesis. I take leave to remind the reader that this is a key-word in our deposits. The dictionary defines its general meaning as 'the recalling of things past'. But what is the nature of this particular recalling? I append the following quotation as being clear and to the point: 'It (anamnesis) is not quite easy to represent accurately in English, words like "remembrance" or "memorial" having for us a connotation of something *absent* which is only mentally recollected. But in the scriptures of both the Old and New Testament *anamnesis* and the cognate verb have a sense of "recalling" or "re-presenting" before God an event in the past so that it becomes *here and now operative by its effects'*. Gregory Dix, *The Shape of the Liturgy*, p. 161.

[2] 'We find an Egyptian king claiming in his coffin-text his identification with Osiris and adding "I am barley".' Eliot Smith, *Human History*, p. 281.

[3] *boneddegion*, bon-eth-ig-yon, th as in nether, accent on penultimate syllable, from *bonedd*, descent. The term is borrowed here from the Welsh laws of the early middle ages, it meant free-born men, and is often qualified by the adjective *cynhwynol*, innate. Today it has the less precise meaning of 'gentlemen'.

[4] *Qui pridie*, the opening words of the prayer of Institution in the Mass 'Who, the day before he suffered, etc.' It is during this prayer that the words of consecration are said, followed by the showing of the sacrament to the people.

blows white on Orcop Hill. [1]
They do say that on this night
                    in the warm byres
shippons, hoggots and out-barns of Britain
in the closes and the pannage-runs and on the sweet lawns of
                                                      Britain
the breathing animals-all [2]
                    do kneel.
Some may say as on this night
                    the narrow grey-rib wolves
from the dark virgin wolds and indigenous thickets of Britain,
though very hungry and already over the fosse, kneel content on the shelving berm.

If these are but grannies' tales
                    maybe that on this night
the nine crones of Glevum in Britannia Prima, [3] and the three
heath-hags that do and do and do
                              north of the Bodotria [4]
in a wild beyond the Agger Antonini
and all the many sisters of Afagddu [5]

---

[1] In 1949 I talked with an elderly Herefordshire farmer who vouched for
the blooming of the thorn. He added that people he knew averred that the cattle
knelt but that that was some long time ago and outside his experience.

[2] Cf. the Christmas carol:
         'Animals all as it befell
         Who were the first to cry nowell.'

[3] Cf. 'the nine witches of Gloucester' that Arthur and his war-band exter-
minated at the Castle of the Wonders in *Peredur son of Efrawg*, the Welsh Percival
tale.

Britannia Prima is here employed merely for convenience, of the Lowland
Zone of Britain, all England is meant. The lines of demarcation between the
provinces of Roman Britain are, I understand, a matter of conjecture.

[4] The Firth of Forth, all Scotland is meant.

[5] Afagddu, av-ág-thee, thus rhyming with Antonini, Sabrina Sea and Dindaethwy. Afagddu was the ugly brother of the beautiful sister, both being children of Ceridwen, a 'nature-goddess', hence of varying attributes. *Afagddu* is
used also as a common noun meaning complete darkness.

that practise transaccidentation from Sabrina Sea
                                        to Dindaethwy[1]
in Mona Insula

                                        tell their *aves*
unreversed.
For these should know, who better?
                        (whose mates
the gossips do say
                        are of the bathosphere)
that the poor mewling babe has other theophanies:
                not then chafed of soiled swaddlings
but with his war-soiled harness tightened on his back.

What says his *mabinogi*?
                Son of Mair, wife of jobbing carpenter
                in via nascitur[2]
                lapped in hay, *parvule*.
But what does his Boast say?
                Alpha es et O
                                that which
                the whole world cannot hold.
                Atheling to the heaven-king.
                Shepherd of Greekland.
                Harrower of Annwn.
                Freer of the Waters.
                Chief Physician and
                dux et pontifex.

---

[1] Dindaethwy, din-daeth-ooy, accent on 'ae' pronounced ah+eh, said
rapidly as a monosyllable. That is to say from the Bristol Channel to Anglesey, all
Wales. Llanddona in the cantred of Dindaethwy, North-East Anglesey, had a
tradition of witches come from Ireland.

[2] See the Homily of St Gregory, Pope, said at matins for Christmas Day.
'Who was not born in the house of his parents but by the wayside (*sed in via
nascitur*) . . . and as though in an alien place.'

Gwledig Nefoedd and
Walda of *every* land
et vocabitur WONDERFUL. ¹

Coming with great power
       Twelve *legiones*, besides auxiliars and flanking *alae*. ²
In that day, *amara valde*³
when she, our Wést-light falls from her tráck-way.
       *Né me pérdas ílla díe*⁴
in that treméndous day
       when Clio has no more to muse about.
When, of the other eight
       Polymnia with Eutérpe alone remain:
how else the Spondaulium⁵ of the Lamb, slain
       *ab origine mundi?*⁶

---

¹ Boast . . . Wonderful.

(A) Cf. 'Cnut rules the land, as Xst the shepherd of Greece, the heavens'.

(B) Annwn, an-noon, the Celtic hades.

(C) Penfeddyg meaning Chief Physician was the title of Peredur, (Percival) who 'freed the waters'. See note 2 to page 225.

(D) Gwledig Nefoedd, goo-led-ig nev-oithe, Ruler of the Heavens. Taliesin addresses God as *gwledig nef a phob tud*, 'ruler of heaven and of every country' or people. Historically the title Gwledig was used only of territorial rulers of importance and its use is confined to the sub- and post-Roman period in Britain.

(E) Walda, Old-English word for ruler, pronounce as in Bretwalda.

(F) See Isaias IX, 6. 'Unto us a child is born . . . and his name shall be called Wonderful.' This is used as the Introit for the Second Mass of Christmas Day.

² See Matt. XXVI, 53.

³ See Office of the Dead, Nocturn III, Versicle.
       '. . . that great and most bitter day.'

⁴ See the hymn *Dies Irae*, verse 9. 'Not me confound in that day.'

⁵ The sacrificial hymn called the Spondaulium was accompanied by flutes; and of the nine muses it is Euterpe, the muse of Lyric poetry, that has the flute.

⁶ See Apocalypse, V. 12, and XIII, 8.

For an anamnesis of whom
is said daily
at the Stone:
hostium i nmaculatam
aberth pur, aberth glân. [1]
Lar of Lares Consitivi
Himself the Lar and the garner
broken under Marmor's sign.
But then, like Marmor *miles*
that whets his weapon acute at both edges. [2]
Out from the mother (coronate of the daughter) [3]
bearing the corn-stalks.
Exact Archon (by whom Astræa on Themis)
Lord-Paraclete of the Assize—
Yet who alone is named MISERICORS.

And who kneels suppliant as yet? Yet they style her Marchioness of the Three Lands and Mundi Domina. [4] This seems much for a creature?

Whose grave eyes are said to be influential, sister, at the

---

[1] *aberth pur, aberth glân*, a pure victim, a holy victim, pronounce approximately ábberrth peerr, ábberrth glahn. They are taken from the modern Welsh rendering of *hostiam puram, hostiam sanctam* in the Mass prayer immediately following the words of consecration. It is in this prayer, that the central achievements of the Victim are commemorated. It begins 'Wherefore . . . calling to mind, etc.' On which account, though the whole Mass is an *anamnesis*, this prayer is especially termed, by liturgists, the Prayer of Anamnesis.

[2] Cf. Apoc., II, 12.
'*Haec dicit qui habet rhomphaeam utraque parte acutam.*'
'These things he says that has the weapon sharp at both its edges.'

[3] See note 1 to page 230 and note 3 to page 231.

[4] Cf. the Mass of the Seven Sorrows, Gradual, '*caeli regina et mundi domina*' and Villon 'Empress of the infernal marsh', and the influence theology predicates to the Mother of God with regard to the fourth land.

Eisteddfa Arbennig[1] in the Gwynfa,[2] where they do already
make ready the chairs for the hidden ones of the Island and
prepare the fillets and chaplets and stitch on the golden
laticlaves for the tunicas of the whole war-band of Theos
Soter, when they shall have come to the guerdon-grove and
unbuckled their dinted loricas?

Where they unbind the remedial rods, Marged![3]

Indeed, and where they shall bare the just axes, my sweet
Mal Fay!

But whose was the fiat six days before the calends of April in
the white *hendref*[4] within the green elbow of the hills, at the
head of the parched Ystrad[5] of the Mercatores in the lower
commot of the cantred of the mixed *gentes* in the tetrarchate
of the Lake of Wonders when Cyrenius was Rhaglaw[6] of the
Three Syrias?

Who rose up and went in haste, mountain-way, through the
middle-land, over the marches twice, into Cantref Iuda[7] in
the ethnarchy of the archeläos, son of the daughter of Isis
queen of cosmocrats,[8] atheling to Herod the Temple, Rex

---

[1] Eisteddfa Arbennig, ei-stéth-vah arr-bén-ig, ei as in height, th as in nether;
principal seat. Historically this was used of the court of the princes of North
Wales at Aberffraw, because, in legal theory, that court was allowed a primacy
of honour over the courts of Powys and the South.

[2] Gwynfa, gwin-vah, paradise, accent on first syllable.

[3] Marged, marr-ged, g hard, Margaret.

[4] *hendref*, hane-drev, permanent homestead.

[5] Ystrad, us-trad, plain.

The Plain of Esdraelon was a world-thoroughfare, toward the north-east end
of which Nazareth is secluded in a semi-circle of small hills.

[6] Rhaglaw, rhymes with vow, it means legate or provincial governor.

[7] Cantref Iuda, can-trev you-da. The accepted English form is 'cantred'.

[8] The mother of the ethnarch of Judaea, son and heir to Herod the Great, is
here confused with Cleopatra the mother of his half-brother Philip and she is
confused with Cleopatra queen of Egypt.

Iudaeorum, son of Edom, son of the Old Adam, father of
foxes; but three months before the advent of the Last Age
of the World¹ in the twenty-ninth of the pontificate of
Caisar Awst² the Conditor sprung of the Strider and
Gwener daughter of the Thunderer, whose old vicar he was?

Dëar me, and who learned you in the historias, the cosmo-
logies and topographies, the genealogies and *nomina*, leaving
aside the rhetorics, sister? Very appetitive ar'n't we?—or
was your knowledge infused?
Or was it in the Greats you read in the meadows of Tŷ
Crist,³ or where are parked the fallow hinds by Pontrhydfodlen,⁴ or within the oriel'd light under the hung dark sword
of the lord Edward o Segeint,⁵ at the cattle-ford, where
sallowed Isis abers with Old Father Tamesis at the Omphalos
and true point of centre of the Island, according to the men-
sural rods and figurings-out of the *gromatici* of the father of
fitz Nut the king in London?

---

¹ When Mary made her journey to visit Elizabeth the latter was already six
months with child. The Last Age of the World was reckoned from the birth of
that child. Thus Nennius says of these world-ages '. . . the fourth from David
to Daniel; the fifth to John the Baptist; the sixth from John to the Judgment
when our Lord Jesus Christ will come to judge the living and the dead, and the
world by fire.'

² Caisar Awst, kei-sar owst, ei as in height, s sibilant, ow as in cow; Caesar
Augustus.

³ Tŷ Crist, tee creest, House of Christ.

⁴ Pontrhydfodlen, pont-rhid-vod-len, accent on penultimate syllable; Bridge
of the Ford of (Mary) Magdalen or Maudlin.

⁵ Edwart o Segeint, ed-wart o seg-eint, ei as in height, accent on first syllable;
Edward of Segontium, who, as Edward II, founded Oriel College. A sword
purporting to be his hangs above his supposed portrait over the high table in
the college hall. My impression on being shown it in 1937 was that it was a very
black sword.

1 Nut, Nudd or Nodens, equates with Lludd, who became 'King Lud' the eponym of London. See *Adventure of Lludd and Llefelys*: 'And a while thereafter Lludd had the Island measured in its length and in its breadth and at Oxford he found the point of centre.' Nudd's son, Edern, a demi-god in Celtic myth, became fitz Nut, the magician, in the Romances.

2 *The A.S. Chronicle* on the character of the Conqueror and the nature of the Great Survey of 1086, says that 'he (William) thought it no shame to do what is shameful to tell'.

3 *Saeson*, saess-on, ae as ah+eh, said as a monosyllable, both esses sibilant, accent on first syllable; the English people.

4 The sack of Ruthin (rith-in) on the eve of the great Fair of St Matthew, in 1400, signalled the Glyn Dŵr revolt. So that the words 'Ruthin Fair' have certain proverbial connotations, comparable to e.g. the words 'Drogheda' or 'Bunker Hill'.

5 Dociau, dok-yi, docks.

6 *môrleidr*, mōrr-lie-derr, accent on first syllable; viking; *môr*, sea, *lleidr* from *latro*.

7 Gynt, gint, g hard, from *gentes*, Scandinavians.
Iwerddon, ee-wer-thon, Ireland. Norwegians were called 'White Heathen', Danes 'Black Heathen'.

8 Pentref (pen-trev) Andes, 'village of Andes', Virgil's actual birthplace near Mantua in Transpadane Gaul.

9 Mari, mah-ree, accent on first syllable, a Welsh colloquial form of Mair or Mary. Very appropriately, the name of Virgil's mother was Maia, the name of the mother of Hermes by Zeus, one of the Pleiades and the name also of the goddess Maia Majesta whose feast was kept on the first day of May, the whole month being sacred to her. Although in the Roman Liturgy no feast of our Lady falls in May, widespread extra-liturgical devotions have christened these ancient pre-Christian associations and the month of May is now popularly known as 'Mary's month'.

10 Mabli, mab-lee, accent on first syllable, Mabel.

11 Ofydd, ov-ith, ith as in hither, Ovid.

12 The modern Welsh word for chemist is a variant of the word *fferyll*, alchemist, or maker, which is simply the name Virgilius, Fferyl (fer-ril), used as a common noun.

13 *Cerdd*, kerrth, th as in nether, song. Eclogue is *bugailgerdd*, shepherd-song.

14 Cf. Virgil, *Ecloga IV*.

15 See the Roman Breviary, at Sext. Versicle. *Elegit eam Deus, et praeelegit eam.*

Now *there* was a survey![1]

Oh, long, long, long before the maid of Falaise brought forth her Devil's *baban*, Gwilim Domesday—who thought no shame to ask what is shame to say.[2]

You see, sister, we are conversant with the annals and are read in *Imago Mundi*, in the chronicle of the *Saeson*,[3] in Prosper and in Isidore, and will, moreover, hear you in Martianus Capella, on the sweet nuptuals of Philologia—

you in y'r stockings of blue!

Where did you pick 'em up, Marged? in Maridunum market or were they salvaged from the cindered booths of Ruthin,[4] or wand-wove are they by the conjurer of Arfon, or was you in Dociau[5] Swansea with a *môrleidr*[6] black, or did you win 'em from the white Gynt[7] of Iwerddon?

We know you get about!

Now sisters! What said our pious father, Maro, Pentref Andes,[8] son of Maia, queen of Mantua, in Gallia Transpadana. There's always a Mari[9] in it, I warrant you!

But fetch the codex, Mabli,[10] No, no, not Ofydd,[11] not the *Ars*—how your mind runs—and we've metamorphoses enough! The *chemist's*[12] book, Mabli, the First Book with the ten shepherd-songs, *cerdd*[13] number four, should be.

Yes, yes, here is it, more or *less*:

Time is already big by sacred commerce with the Timeless courses. Fore-chose and lode-bright, here is the maiden, Equity! The chthonic old Sower restores the Wastelands. The First-Begotten, of the *caer* of heaven (which is a long way off!), would bring his new orient down for our alignment.[14]

Sisters, not so jealous! *Someone* must be chosen and fore-chosen[15]—it stands to reason! After all there should be

[213]

solidarity in woman. No great thing but what there's a woman behind it, sisters. Begetters of all huge endeavour we are. The Lord God may well do all without the aid of man,[1] but even in the things of god a woman is medial—it stands to reason. Even the gigantic *dynion gynt*[2] and mighty tyrannoi of old time must needs have had mortal woman for mothers, if demi-gods or whatever father'd 'em—it stand-to reason. For these were of flesh and bone, not illusions men. So here also there is occasion for very flesh, for how should the eternal hypostases be conjoined with a flesh not substantial?

Expert with the *hudlath*[3] we may be, and professionally concerned with many and various metamorphoses, p'r'aps, but not Docetae,[4] I hope!

It all hangs on the fiat. If her fiat was the Great Fiat, nevertheless, seeing the solidarity, we participate in the fiat—or can indeed, by our fiats—it stands to reason. Not chosen and forechosen of Theos Soter, indeed, but not so jealous, sisters: there is proportions and magnitudes and degrees both of conferrings and of acceptances, very and many various, and, after all, sisters, he was her *baban*.[5]

Who did him wash
and did his swaddlings wring?
Who did and mended for him?
Who repaired for him his tunic of one weave
now in Treventum?—so it is said.

---

[1] Cf. English carol
'Who all without the aid of man
Bore us the King of Kings.'
[2] *dynion gynt*, din-yon gint, men of by-gone times.
[3] *hudlath*, hid-lahth, magician's wand; from *hud*, illusion and *llath*, rod.
[4] The Docetic doctrine was that our Lord had only an apparent or phantom body. Magicians or such as deal with occult knowledge, of any time or place, tend toward such Mandæan or Manichee-like beliefs.
[5] *baban*, bab-ban, accent on first syllable, babe.

Of whom was his mother-wit?
Who was of the gladius transfixed?

                    Whose psyche
was alone found patient of such transfixion
in all the world?

        Wherefore we malkins three
for all our sisters
        of Anglia et Walliae and of Albany
our un-witched *aves* pay
        if only on this, HER NIGHT OF ALL.
Unto the bairn, as three clerks inclining
when they confess themselves before his Stone
at the Introit-time.[1]

             Kneel sisters!
             Graymalkin! Kneel.
Kneel my sweet ape
         whose habit is to imitate.
For in the Schools, they say:
         if he but take the posture
the old grey ass may bray a *Gloria*.

If much of this is fancy-fed though not unmixed with some
theology, more surely on this night the white owls of Britain,

---

[1] Cf. Dunbar. *On the Nativity of Christ.*
      'All clergy do to him inclyne
      And bow unto that bairn benying.'
  Cf. also how at the beginning of Mass, during the singing of the Introit by the
choir, the *Confiteor* is said at the steps of the altar, first by the celebrant alone
to the deacon and sub-deacon, and then by these, as representing all those
present, to the celebrant.

seeking ·their Lady Wisdom where the columned Purbeck
gleams, would find her under Pales' thack, *ad praesepem.* [1]

                     If this, though sure, is but allegory

at all events

                 and speaking most factually

and, as the fashion now requires, from observed data: On
this night, when I was a young man in France, in Gallia
Belgica, the forward ballista-teams of the Island of Britain
green-garlanded their silent three-o-threes [2] for this I saw
and heard their cockney song salute the happy morning; and
later, on this same morning certain of the footmen of Britain,
walking in daylight, upright, through the lanes of the war-net
to outside and beyond the rusted trip-belt, some with gifts,
none with ported weapons, embraced him between his *fossa*
and ours, exchanging tokens.

                          And this I know,
if only from immediate hearsay, for we had come on this
mild morning (it was a Green Christmas) back into the rear,
two to three thousand paces behind where his front *vallum*
was called by us, the Maiden's Bulge, and ours, the Pontiff's
Neb, between which parallels, [3] these things, according to
oral report reaching us in this forward reserve area, were done,
                  BECAUSE OF THE CHILD.

This is the night

                    when the second official
wearing his best orphrey'd jacket, must sing from his *Liber*

---

   [1] Cf. carol

        In dulci jubilo now sing we all I.O.
        He my love my wonder lieth *in praesepio*

   [2] More usually known as 'eighteen pounders'.

   [3] The allusions are reflective of names given to salient features of the opposing
trench lines in the Richebourg sector in 1915; e.g. Gretchen's Trench, Sally
Trench, the Pope's Nose, Sophia's Trench and the Neb.

Mandatorum[1] (which is the New Mandate) the beginning of the *mabinogi*[2] of the Maban the Pantocrator, the true and eternal Maponos, and of . . . Rhiannon[3] of the bird-throats, was it? Spouse of the lord of Faëry? Matrona of the Calumniations, seven winters at the horse-block telling her own *mabinogi* of detraction?

Modron our mother?

Ein mam hawddgar?[4]

Truly!

that we must now call MAIR,[5]

---

[1] Certain high officials of the later Imperial Roman civil service received as part of their insignia a book of words called the *Liber Mandatorum*; it has been suggested that the ceremonial (lights and incense) attaching to these magistrates and their insignia, passed on to the chief officers of the Christian church or their representatives and that subsequently the book of the New Law, the Gospels, being as it were in place of the secular instruments, came to be honoured with a like ceremonial.

[2] *Mabinogi*, mab-in-og-ee, accent on third syllable. Cf. note 5 to page 200 above. Maban, infant. Maponos the Celtic god equated with Apollo who equates in certain aspects with our Lord.

[3] Rhiannon (rhee-an-non) is essentially a mother-figure, in fact the Great Mother, Ragantona. She gave birth to the Great Son; long penance was inflicted on her unjustly and the song of her celestial birds is still proverbial in Wales. Her lover was Arawn king of the Otherworld, though the whole motif is so very dislocated in the redaction of the myth surviving in the *Mabinogion* as to be unrecognizable.

[4] *Ein mam hawddgar*, ein (ei as in height) mahm howthe-garr. 'Our Mater Amabilis', see the Welsh translation of the Litanies of Mary. Welshmen tell me that *hawddgar* equates very accurately with the Latin *amabilis* for *hawddgar* implies loveliness and comeliness together with a buxomness of spirit; meanings lost in our English translation 'Mother most amiable'.

[5] The Latin name Maria gives Mair in Welsh; approximately mah-eer pronounced as a monosyllable but with emphasis on the first vowel.

So that this form of this crucial name, connects us directly with the first introduction of our religion among the peoples of this island. For the Romano-British Latin-speaking provincials Mary would be Maria. But *Meir* (now spelt Mair) was the first vernacular form of the name of the Mother of God used when the Celtic language was devolving into Early Welsh, during the Roman Occupation. We English-speaking persons are familiar with Mair owing to the many place-names beginning with Llanfair—, i.e. 'Mary's Church' or rather 'Mary's enclosure', or, best of all, the exact etymon, 'Maryland'. Cf. note 4 to page 185 above.

NOTES TO PAGE 219

1 Bride, Ffraid, Brig, Brigantia, Brigit, a kind of Celtic Vesta; her fire-rites became later associated with St Brigit of Kildare called 'the Mary of the Gael', Secondary Patron of All Ireland, whose feast is on February 1 the Eve of Candlemas. Romano-British dedications to the goddess Brigantia have been identified in London, Cheshire and Scotland. Bride is the accepted English form as in St Bride's and the Bridewell.

2 The Gospel for the first Mass of Christmas begins with 'A decree went out from Caesar Augustus' and ends with 'to men of good will'.

3 The Second Legion, called 'Augustus's Own', had long-standing associations with us; it was stationed at Caerleon-on-Usk for 300 years, and at Richborough in Kent for 65 years. Its tradition must have been very 'Anglo-Indian' indeed.

4 See Virgil, *Eclogue IV*, lines 6 and 10, 'Now also the Virgin returns'. 'Now Apollo reigns'. I had especially in mind a palimpsest in which the large letters of Cicero's *De Republica* are still plainly visible beneath the smaller, fluent, clear uncials of St Augustine's Commentary on the Psalms, owing to ineffective erasion. The seven existing MSS of Virgil are in evenly spaced, dressed lines of square or rustic capitals.

5 The Last Age of the World was reckoned from the birth of John the Baptist. It was he who stole the Mid-Summer Fires from Servius Tullius, son of Vulcan the Smith.

6 *Imperator* gave *ameraudur* in earlier Welsh, now spelt *ymherawdr* (um-her-row-der) accent as in the Latin original. Like the word Mair (see note 5 to page 217) this word also connects us directly with Roman Britain. It must have been heard in some similar form over much of Britain during the first half millenium AD. It must have been heard sometimes in the streets of Latin-speaking cosmopolitan Roman London.

7 It will be recalled that Venus apart from her title *Genetrix* as Mother of the Roman state had also the other titles, *Cloacina* and *Verticordia* which can be seen as corollaries of the first title, for it was under these titles that she was supplicated as guardian of nuptial fidelity. It is an aspect of Venus-worship glossed over by the Romantic tradition, but it was there and is part of our deposit.

8 Pencawr pen-kowrr (as in cow), head giant, or chief tyrranus.

9 *palas*, pal-lass, accent on first syllable, palace.

10 Maban, mab-ban, accent on first syllable, male child.

11 *englynion*, en-glun-yon. Strictly speaking this refers to stanzas of a particular construction, but I use it here of the angel's song because had that message a Welsh mythological setting, the song would have been in the form of an *englyn*. The reader will be familiar with the expression, 'Then he sang this englyn' in Lady Guest's *Mabinogion*; it is as though to say 'prose does not meet the case'.

12 Cf. Mass, Preface for Christmas, *cumque omni militia caelestis exercitus*.

IAM·REDIT·APOLLO·IAM

REDIT · ET VIRGO
EXIIT EDICT
VM A CAESAR
E AVGVSTO·
ET PEPERIT·
FILIVM SV
VM PRIMO
GENITVM·
ET RECLINAVIT·
EVM IN PRAESEPIO
ET HOC VOBIS SIGNVM

She that makes the gillies of Bride of the februal Fires[1]
gillies of her Son
                              whose spouses we are all
as be naiad-signed.
But first, careful that his right thumb is touching the letters
of the writing, he must make the sign, down and across,
beginning where the imposed, preclear-bright uncial reads,
Exiit edictum a Caesare Augusto.[2]
Just where, in a goodish light, you can figure-out the ghost-
capitals of indelible eclogarii, rectilineal, dressed by the left,
like veterani of the Second,[3] come again to show us how,
from far side shadowy Acheron and read
IAM REDIT . . VIRGO
                    . . . . IAM REGNAT APOLLO[4]

And then he must (after he has joined his hands together)
relate in a clear high voice from this Aramaean brut, of how
that within six months[5] from the beginning of the Sixth Age
of the World, our divine Ymherawdr[6] Octavian, ever august,
of the blood of the progenitress the Purifier, Turner of
Hearts[7] and of Mars Pencawr[8] (the *old* Pantocrator) seated
in curia, in his ivory chair, with his cushion under him, in
the apsed hall of his *palas*[9] on the Caelian heights that sur-
mount the earth, sent out a decree, demanding his heriots,
man-fees and entertainment-dues from the free-trevs and the
bond-trevs of all the cantrevs of the whole universal orbis,
and of how the wolf-watch in the lower-field (for it was
winter calends) because of certain marvels, understood where
to find the Maban.[10]

                    But when he comes to the end
of the heavenly *englynion*[11] that the poor men from the
villein-trev heard the messenger that brought the amnesty
and with him the bright-mailed war-band of full complement,[12] sing in Latin (that is to say at the word *voluntatis*),

however much he would wish to continue proclaiming his wonder-tale, he must break off the recitation of this true *historia* and be silent.

For the *textus* must be taken back to the Stone, because the court-*capelwr*[1] (who is offerant on this night) is waiting, by the Stone, to kiss the *textus*, and to say into it, quietly, this couplet:

> *Per evangelica dicta*
> *Deleantur nostra delicta.*[2]

This is the night for which the Master of the Children has tried since Clemens and Felicity to learn his nudging boys to say properly—in brogued Goidel Vulgate

> *Laetentur coeli.*[3]

The night when they begin
            at May Major
in pontiff's sung-nasal

> *Dominus dixit ad me.*[4]

But when they come to Anastasia
            and fetching Hemera early from her bed

---

[1] *capelwr*, chaplain, cap-pel-oorr, accent on middle syllable.

[2] 'By the words of the gospel may our faults be blotted out.' See the rubric directing what is to be done after the singing of the gospel: 'The sub-deacon takes the book to the priest who kisses the Gospel and says' *Per evangelica*, etc., as above quoted. The g in *evangelica* is to be soft.

[3] See the First Mass of Christmas, sung at midnight from St Mary Major on the Esquiline Hill. Offertory, 'Let the heavens rejoice and let the earth be glad, etc.' Cf. the existence of Christianized Goidels (Irish) at e.g. Silchester, Hants, in the fifth century.

[4] Ibid. Introit, 'The Lord said unto me thou art my son, this day have I begotten thee.'
The *main* liturgical emphasis in this first Mass is on the physical birth of a child in time and at a specified site.

(for she to welcome him must surely gaud with her dawn-
blush reds the wither of the year, nor do less in awe to him
than do poor Hobs with aid-fires)[1]
is it they?

       or clear-voiced cantors

tunicled as though
in cloth of rainbow

       (from the wide-pomoerium'd Urbs
as ultramundane to the Pleiades as to the ordered polis whose
archetype the Pleiad is)
that sing and say

         Lux fulgebit hodie?[2]

Keeping this most stella'd night
on Christmas Day in the Morning.
Then back to Mary Major to hear them tell of how that from
before all time Minerva is sprung from the head of Jove.[3]

    *   *   *

[1] Cf. Milton, *Hymn on the Morning of Christ's Nativity*, Verse I.
    'Nature in aw to him
    Had doff't her gawdy trim
     With her great Master so to sympathize'.

[2] See the Second Mass of Christmas; Introit, Isaias IX. 'A light shall shine
upon this day, etc.' This Mass, called Aurora Mass, is sung at daybreak from the
church of St Anastasia on the Palatine Hill, formerly the chapel royal of the
emperors. In this Mass it is not so much the birth that is celebrated as the
radiance which the birth sheds on the world-darkness.

[3] The Third Mass of Christmas is said, like the first, from St Mary Major,
but the emphasis is now on the timeless begetting of the Logos which alone
makes sense of this particular birth in time.
  Cf. also *Minerva Jovis capite orta* as a formula proposed by one of the pontiffs
to express the Eternal Generation of the Word, but, for various reasons, not
officially adopted.

VIII

SHERTHURSDAYE AND VENUS DAY

SHERTHURSDAYE AND VENUS DAY

He that was her son
is now her lover
signed with the quest-sign
at the down-rusher's ford. [1]
Bough-bearer, harrower [2]
torrent-drinker, [3] *restitutor*.

He, by way of her
of her his gristle and his mother-wit.
White and ruddy her
beautiful in his shirt
errant for her now
his limbs like pillars. [4]

Her Thursday's child
come far to drink his Thor's Day cup: [5]
At night, within
at his lit board.
Without in the night-grove
far side the torrent-bed
and on Gwener's morning
on Skull Mountain.
Marquis of demarking waters
Warden of the Four Lands

---

[1] Cf. the meaning of Jordan, 'down-rusher', according to G. Adam Smith in *Hist. Geo. of the Holy Land*.

[2] Cf. the theme which is first referred to in Peter's first epistle 'he went and preached to the spirits in prison'; and which is made credal in 'he descended into hell', and which was elaborated in fourth-century apocryphal writings from which the medieval miracle plays entitled 'The Harrowing of Hell' drew part of their material.

[3] Cf. Ps. *Dixit Dominus*, last verse, 'He shall drink of the brook (*torrente*) in the way'.

[4] Cf. Isaias LXIII, 7. (Vul.) *iste formosus in stola sua* and Song of Songs, V, 10 and 15 (A.V.).

[5] See the Nursery Rhyme: *Monday's Child*, line 4, 'Thursday's child has far to go'.

from her salined deeps
from the cavern'd waters
        (where she ark'd him) come.
      His members in-folded
like the hidden lords in the West-tumuli
for the nine dark calends gone.
Grown in stature
              he frees the waters.
(Nine nights on the windy tree?[1]
              Himself to himself?
Who made the runes would read them—
              wounded with *our* spears.)
Her Peredur
     vagrant-born, earth-fostered
acquainted with the uninhabited sites.
          His woodland play is done, he has seen the
questing *milites*, he would be a *miles* too.[2]
              Suitor, margaron-gainer.

---

[1] Cf.   'I know that I hung on the windy tree
       For nine whole nights
       Wounded with the spear, dedicated to Odin,
       Myself to myself.'
From *The Havamal*, as translated by Frazer in *Adonis, Attis, Osiris*.

[2] 'Peredur . . . *miles* too.' (Per-red-eerr, accent on middle syllable.)
The allusions are to the opening episode, concerning the hero and his mother in the Welsh story of *Peredur son of Efrawg*, called Peredur the Chief Physician. He is the hero known to all Europeans as Percival, *the* Grail hero, after the original Gawain and before a much later development of that complicated theme evolved a Galahad. Peredur was nurtured in a remote place by his mother who kept all knowledge of arms from him, but playing in the woods he sees military persons pass by and inquires what they are, and is told 'Angels'. He answers 'I would be an angel too' and attaches himself to them. His mother swoons in sorrow. He goes on his quest, frees and restores the Wasteland: the streams flow again, marriages are consummated and the earth fructifies. See also note 3 (C) to page 208 above.

Tryst-keeper
>   his twelve-month-and-a-day
falls tomorrow.
He would put on his *man's* lorica.
>   He has put it on
his *caligae* on
>   and is gone
to the mark-land.
Unless his two-edged gladius gain it
>   what tillage is there
for the *Volk*?
Unless he ask the question[1]
>   how shall the rivers run
or the suitors persuade their loves
or the erosion of the land cease?
What more should he do
>   that he hasn't done?[2]
>   His dispositions made
he would at once begin the action.
He has begun it
>   here
within the camp
>   see
>   he takes the auguries.
How else the dawn deployment?
What shapes else the quarter-less contact
>   at the mound?

---

[1] The reference is to the Percival story concerning the consequences attendant upon the failure of the hero to 'ask the question'. See *The Mabinogion*, translated Gwyn and Thomas Jones, *Everyman* edtn 1949, p. 218. For a full discussion of the task of the hero see *From Ritual to Romance*, Ch. II, Jessie Weston, Cambridge, 1920.

[2] Cf. the Good Friday Liturgy, the Adoration of the Cross, Versicle, *Quid ultra etc.* 'What more ought I to do for thee and have not done it'.

There are but children, weak:
these cannot tell what mound-war means. [1]
For these:
down the long history-paths
in the quiet apses
where it's very still
the fracture-sound
when
with this hand and that hand conjoined
over the poured-out confluence
he parts that, [2] which—
under the sign of that creature—
can do more than any grain. [3]
All have stomach for these comfortable signs
in the lighted apses.

Within, with lights brighted
under the dressed beam
all can eat the barley-cake
and sisters dear
may plait him bearded
for their hair
and all can sing:
Fol the dol the didiay

---

[1] Cf. C. F. Alexander, *We are but Little Children Weak*, and, by the same author, *There is a Green Hill*, verse 2,
'. . . we cannot tell what pains he had to bear'.
[2] Cf. the Mass rubric, 'he takes the host into both hands and breaks it down the middle over the chalice'.
[3] Cf. the folk-song, *John Barleycorn*, last verse:
'It will do more than any grain By the turning of your hand'.

but he
             he must be broken off at knee. [1]
Within, in the lighted *sacellum* [2]
as yet the *signum*
                        shorn soon
                        draggled at Black Fosse [3]
                        lopped at the *agger*
stands dressed—reg'mental
                        and the binding *sacramentum* [4]
is reaffirmed upon it.
Down the traversed history-paths
             his stumbling *Grenadiere*
in the communication-ways
                        his burdened infants
shall learn like vows to take.

As a *paterfamilias* among his own on his own festal-night

---

[1] Ibid, verse 5.
             'Then they sent men with scythes so sharp
             To cut him off at knee
             And then poor Johnny Barleycorn
             They served him barbarously.
             Chorus: Fol the dol the didiay
                        Fol the dol the diddy aggy woo.'
[2] The chapel in the praetorium of any legionary camp in which the standards were kept and venerated.
[3] Cf. the meaning of the name Cedron 'the black torrent'. When dry this water-course is a squalid ditch like a fosse below the east wall of the city; at least, that is the kind of memory I have of it—there is also the ancient tradition that our Lord stumbled and fell into a runnel or ditch in this vicinity when being brought captive from Gethsemane.
[4] Cf. the *sacramentum*, the oath of allegiance in the Roman army, with which the Christian use of the word has certain affinities.

empties out to the Genius of the place[1]

he in this place

empties himself

to the Lar of this place

of this household

in session, here

under the roof-beam at the bright hearth of

this Lar.

Here, to the Genius of this *familia* of new-*gens* founders

inaugurally met.

Informed from before history proper:

from the boundary-time.

They say that, once-upon-a-time, there was a duke without tree

the stirpless lord, a man of estate *sine genealogia*

a rites-offerant

of an immutable *disciplina*.

Rex Pacis was his name

gentle, was his station.[2]

Out from his dwelling place[3]

to the tithing of the spoil

to take his war-dues.[4]

---

[1] Cf. the Roman domestic rites on the birthday of the head of the house which was also the chief festival of the *genius* of the household. In making the oblations the father offered in fact to his *own* Genius, to the 'indwelling spirit that gave the father of the family the power to prolong its existence'. H. Stuart Jones, *Companion to Roman History*.

[2] Cf. Heb. VII, 4 (A.V.), 'consider how great this man was'.

[3] Cf., e.g.

> Alice Bradshaw is my name
> Simple is my station
> Rotherhithe my dwelling place
> And Christ my salvation.

[4] Gen. XIV, 20.

Our chrism'd Triptolemus
to quicken, to judge:

           the furrows
           the dead
from dear and grave Demeter come
           germ of all:
of the dear arts as well as bread.
To institute, to make stable
to offer oblations

           permanent
kindly, acceptable and valid:
           tillage fruit
           man's-norm
then rational
           so food of angels. [1]

Munera

           of Liber, poured
           of Ceres, broken.
Not desert-rites, nor nomad-*liberi*. [2]
Levites! the new rite holds
           is here
before your older rites begin. [3]

---

[1] Cf. '*Ecce panis angelorum*' and 'man is . . . Reasonable as an Aungell.'

Triptolemus was sent by the Mother Goddess to initiate agriculture and settled civilization and was also at Eleusis judge of the dead. He necessarily recalls Melchesidec who appears as a priest of agriculture-rites in a pastoral setting at the termination of a tribal war. If the significance of such types was brought out by the author of Hebrews VII, the Roman liturgists from very early on had given that significance special point and emphasis by relating it very immediately to the manual act of sacrifice, so that it continues still to be reasserted, every day, wherever a priest of the Roman rite asks that his offering of the transubstantiated fruits of the earth shall be identified with and as acceptable as 'that which thy high priest Melchesidec offered up to thee'. (See the Roman Mass prayer *Supra quae propitio*, following close on the act of consecration.)

[2] In the sense of the young of animals.

[3] Cf. Heb. VII, 5-11 and the Maundy Thursday hymn, *Pange lingua*, verse 5.
'*Et antiquum documentum Novo cedat ritui*' 'And let an antique formula give place to a new rite.'

Here.
Where?
                    Here when?
Here at the spoil-dump
at a war's term
where the high-flyer stalls
                    after his concentric
and exact reconnaissance. [1]

Not every year is the salvage of so many inhabited places
made legitimate loot. Not at every time are the cosmocrats
as prodigal or the bleached bodies so many, as now, in this
place.
In the wasted land
                    at jackal-meet
at the division of the spoils
with his hands stretched out
                    he continues. [2]

Failing
                    (finished?) West
          your food, once.
Upon a time
                    the Daughter's torch
                    Demeter's arch [3]

---

[1] Cf. the name of the hawk-headed god Horus which is said to mean 'high-
flyer'. I was thinking of the mis-called 'eagles' that I saw in Egypt which seem
to stand still at a great height before they drop on something they have sighted.

[2] See *Extensis manibus prosequitur*, the words of the rubric directing the posture
of the celebrant at the prayer in the mass beginning *Supra quae propitio*.

[3] Persephone associated with her mother Demeter in sending forth Triptolemus to teach man agriculture and the arts of civilization.

See note 1 to page 230 above.

extinguished
down
              in our streets
where is corn and wine?[1]

Calling to mind the ancient precept
                    the night-mandate
to the wanderer-duke
          the fidell alien-sire *fidelium*
he, *nemorensis*, between the maritime flats and the foot-hills
on his ordeal-night
when it was said to him
              out of Bersabee night-vault:
Take the lamb that you do love
          —his mother's boy
get north-east by north
          by way of Liknites'[2] cave of bread, past anemone-

---

[1] See *Tenebrae* for Good Friday 1st Nocturn, Lesson 2. '*Ubi est triticum et vinum . . . in plateis civitatis.*' Lamentations II, 12.

[2] Cf. the O.T. narrative: 'And Abraham planted a grove in Beer-sheba (Vul. *plantavit nemus in Bersabee*) and called on the name of the Lord. . . . Take now thy son, thine only son Isaac whom thou lovest and get thee into the land of Moriah; and offer him there for a burnt offering upon one of the mountains which I will tell thee of.' (Gen. XXI, 33 and XXII, 2, A.V.) For 'get thee into the land of Moriah' Vulgate reads *vade in terram visionis;* this 'land of vision' is the 'high place' of the Jebusites, called Mount Moriah, that is to say part of the site on which Jerusalem subsequently stood and to get to it from Beersheba one would, and the ancient track did, go via Bethlehem (House of Bread, or with equal significance *Beit Laham*, House of Flesh), a place sacred to Adonis for whom *Es Sitt*, 'the lady' (in this case Ishtar), weeps. The anemones in part of Palestine are still said to be red with his blood that was shed by the boar's tusks. The name Liknites was applied to Dionysius and other cult-figures and could signify 'crib-born'.

dell where poor Ishtar is a-weeping in the burning sun of day
     where her precious
bloods the flowery carpet she shall kneel
    at the turn of the hog-track.
Up by the parched concentric bends over the carious de-
marcations between the tawny ramps and the gone-fallow
lynchets
        into vision-lands.
On to one of the mountains there
       on an indicated hill
not on any hill
     but on Ariel Hill
that is as three green hills of Tegeingl [1]
in one:
     the hill of the out-cry
     the hill of dereliction
     the *moel* of the *mamau* [2]
that is all help-heights
the mound of the in-cries.
Of which cry?
    His, by whom all oreogenesis is
his hill-cry who cries from his own *oreos*.
      Ante colles he is and
before the fleeting hills
      in changing order stood.

---

[1] Tegeingl, teg-ine-gl, stress accent on *first* syllable, gl as gle in angle.
There are three hills of which my father used to speak to be seen from the vicinity of his birthplace in that part of Wales once called Tegeingl, now called Flintshire. Y Foel-y-Crio, the Hill of the Cry, Moel Famau, Hill of the Mothers, and Moel Ffagnallt, which I was once told signified hill of despair or dereliction, but I can find no confirmation of this supposed meaning nor anything resembling it. As, however, that is the meaning I associated with it from an early age, and as it has become integrated with the text I shall retain it.

[2] *moel*, moil, hill; *mamau*, mothers. As has already been noted, the Welsh *au* rhymes with the ei in heights, and in this case has assonance with 'out-cry' and 'in-cries'.

1 Cf. 'Before the hills was I brought forth', Pro. VIII, 25, said of Wisdom and applied in the Liturgy to the Mother of God who represents Wisdom. She was quickened by the Spirit and the bringer forth of the Logos-made-Flesh. Or, to use a mythologer's terms, she is both bride and mother of the cult-hero.

Cf. also 'she shall laugh in the latter day', said of the 'valiant woman' in Pro. XXXI, 25, in the Douay version.

2 Cf.
> 'At twelve years old he talked with men
> The Jews all wondering stand
> Yet he obeyed his mother then
> And came at her command.'

3 Cf. English folk-song:
> 'On yonder hill there stands a creature
> Who she is I do not know
> I'll go court her for her beauty'

And the nursery rhyme, *Simple Simon*:
> 'All the water he had got
> Was in his mother's pail.'

And the title '*Feoderis Arca*' in the Litanies of Mary.

4 Cf. the Liturgy for Holy Saturday, the Blessing of the Font, *Qui te de paradisi* etc. 'Who made thee flow from the fountain of paradise and commanded thee to water the whole earth with thy four rivers.'

5 Gwenfrewi, better known as Winefred, the well-saint of Holywell, Flints. Pronounce, approx. gwen-vruh-we, accent on middle syllable.

6 Drayton speaks of St David drinking of the 'crystal Hodni'. This is the same river as the Honddu after which Llanthony is named. Llan Dewi Nant Honddu, the 'enclosure of David in the dingle of the Honddu'. This stream is crystal clear and its banks are ferny. David had a cell there.

7 Dyfrdwy is the Welsh name of the Dee; pronounce, dovrr-dooy, ov as in gov'nor, accent on first syllable.

Dyfrwr, dove-róorr, accent on first syllable. Y Dyfrwr is the Welsh word for Aquarius, and St David is called Dewi Ddyfrwr, David the Waterman.

8 Cf. the Blessing of the Font, '*sit haec sancta et innocens creatura*'.

9 Cf. the prayer used for the blessing of holy water 'who . . . hast appointed water to be the foundation of thy greatest sacraments'.

10 Cf. Dunbar 'Hevins distil your balmy schouris' and the *Benedicite*, 'every shower and dew'.

11 Cf. Blessing of Font, 'by that God who in the beginning separated thee from the dry land' (*ab arida*) and also the words *simplices* and *foecundet* used of the water and *primordia* used of the world in the same rite.

12 Cf. Hopkins: 'As tumbled over rim in roundy wells
    Stones ring . . .'

He by whom is she to whom by a wise allegory they make
apply, *ante colles ego parturiebar*: she that laughs last. [1]
Sophia's child that calls him master
he her groom that is his mother.
Her's who at twelve years taught men:

                      the sophists wonder

where they stand. [2]

                      Stands a lady

on a mountain

                      who she is

they could not know.
His waters were in her pail
her federal waters ark'd him. [3]
He by whom the welling *fontes*
           are from his paradise-font mandated[4]
to make virid Gwenfrewi's[5] glen, Dyfrdwy
to crystal his ferned Hodni[6] dell
               dewy for the Dyfrwr[7]
by this preclear and innocent creature. [8]
He whose greater signs are
             per creaturam aquam[9]
he of all the schouris balm
               and every dew[10]

continually.
Who primordially separated
            this simple and fecund creature

ab arida. [11]
Mandater of all the roundy-wells[12]
           totius orbis mundi
loosener of the naiad-girdles
(how else his valid matter

[235]

for the sign-stream?) [1]
Praefect of the strict conduits, but
by him the wild-brooks [2]
all the *humida Telluris*

every distillation

toto orbe terrarum. [3]
Arglwydd [4] of the Fountain
Magister of the Cisterns

whose voice is:

tamquam vox aquarum.

(When at the imagined corners
his salpinx'd *Diktat* is:

Uncover everything! [5])

As the many voices of them.

Of all the clamant waters

---

[1] The references are: to the term 'valid matter' used by theologians of the material water in the Sacrament of Water; to the material water essential to the Sacrament of Bread and Wine; to the water-metaphor used of all the seven signs; to the entire sign-world to which the metaphor of water flowing from a common source could apply; to the actual streams, our rivers, which are themselves signs of conveyance and themselves physically convey, which not only provide the metaphors but the material stuff without which the sacraments could not be.

[2] Accent on 'wild', cf. the West-Sussex locality-name 'the Wild Brooks'.

[3] See the Blessing of the Font: 'Who opens the fonts of baptism in the whole earth' (*toto orbe terrarum*).

[4] Arglwydd, Lord, pronounce arr-glooith, ith as in dither, accent on first syllable. Cf. *Arglwyddes y Ffynnon*, The Lady of the Fountain, the Welsh romance-tale corresponding with the European romance *Le Chevalier au Lion*.

[5] See Donne.

'At the round earth's imagin'd corners, blow
Your trumpets, Angells ...'
and Apocalypse I, 15. Vul. and A.V.

[236]

firthing forth from the Four Avons
        himself the *afon*-head. [1]
        His cry
from the axile stipe
        at the dry node-height
when the dark cloud brights the trembling lime-rock.
(All known clouds distil showers.
Is there no water in that dark cloud
           for the parched lime-face?
What unknown cloud then, is this?)

As the bleat of the spent stag
          toward the river-course
he, the *fons*-head
          pleading, *ad fontes*
his desiderate cry: [2]

              SITIO. [3]

              What will the naiads
do now, poor things:
             the lady of the *ffynnon* [4]

---

[1] Avons, pronounced as in Stratford-on-Avon, whereas *afon* is pronounced av-von, the Welsh common noun, meaning a river, from which 'Avon' derives. And cf. Gen. II, 10.

[2] Cf. the psalm. '*Quemadmodum desiderat cervus ad fontes aquarum.*' (Vul. Ps. 41.)

'Like as the hart desireth the water-brooks.' (Bk. of Com. Pr. Ps. 42.)

Fel y brefa'r hydd am yr afonydd dyfroedd. As the bleat of the stag for the rivers of waters. (Welsh Psalter).

[3] I found myself having to use the Latin *sitio* for the English 'I thirst', because that is the form most impressed upon me by hearing the ministers singing the passion on Good Friday. Three pitches are used by three separate cantors: a high pitch for words said by Pilate, the priests, etc., a middle pitch for the narrative and a deep pitch for the words attributed to our Lord. *Sitio* is sung to six notes, G G A G F F. See illustration facing p. 235.

[4] *ffynnon*, fun-non, fountain, from *fontana*.

Es Sitt that moves the *birket*, ¹ fays *del lac*, the donnas of the lyn, ² the triad-*matres*, the barley-tressed *mamau*³ and the grey-eyed *nymphae* at the dry *ffynhonnau* whose *silvae*-office is to sing: ⁴

VNVS HOMO NOBIS

(PER AQVAM)

RESTITVIS REM. ⁵

But tell me his cry
            no, his cry before his *mors*-cry.
Of his black-hoürs' cryings
            his ninth hour out-cry. . . . ⁶

---

¹ *Es Sitt*, The Lady; *birket*, pool, as in Birket sitti Miriam, Pool of the Lady Mary, the Arab name for the Pool of Bethesda where the 'angel went down . . . and troubled the water', in John's gospel.

² lyn, an anglicization of *llyn*, a water. Cf. Lynton?

³ It has already been noted that the treble goddesses, the Deae Matres of antiquity, may have given the name *mamau*, mothers, to the fairies in Wales.

⁴ Because the Welsh *au* approximates to the English ei in height, the words *mamau* (mothers) and *ffynhonnau* (fountains) rhyme with elements in the English words naiad, grey-eyed and triad, and with the Latin *ae* in *nymphae* (nymphs) and *silvae* (of a woodland).

⁵ 'One man, by water, restores to us our state' (i.e. continues to restore).

As a certain amount of 'unshared background' directed me here, I shall relate as follows: Some thirty-five years ago, in Wales, the water-supply of the house in which I was staying, was, on Christmas Eve, diverted at the source, which made it necessary for my friend, Mr René Hague, and myself to go by night to where the mountain-stream was deliberately blocked and to free the water. On our return journey Mr Hague remarked '*Duo homines per aquam nobis restituerunt rem*'. He then told me of the famous line of Ennius adapted by Virgil. In writing my text I found that Mr Hague's impromptu variation (with the singular number restored) was exactly what I required. Cf. Ennius. *Unus homo nobis cunctando restituit rem*. 'One man by delaying restored to us our state.' Cf. Virgil. *Unus qui nobis cunctando restituis rem*. 'You who alone by delaying restore to us our state.'

⁶ Cf. Matt. XXVII, 46. Cf. also G. M. Hopkins.
            'I wake and feel the fell of dark, not day
            What hours, O what black hoürs we have spent.'

At the taking over of third day-relief[1]
                             three hours since
the median hour.

            (On the keels-roads
on her sea who is lode of it
they would be sounding six bells
                    and the first dog-watch relief
can bide a full hour yet.)[2]

It is the empty time
                    after tiffin
and before his first stiff peg.
The fact-man, Europa's vicar
the Samnite of the Pontian *gens*[3]
within the conditioned room
                             sleeps on
secure under the tiffany.
                    They sting like death
at afternoon.

---

[1] When I wrote this I was under the impression that one of the routine hours for changing guard in the Roman army was 3 p.m.

[2] At sea the first dog-watch or half-watch is from 4 p.m. to 6 p.m. Cf. page 96 above, 'What bells is that, etc.'
The synoptic gospels agree that our Lord died at 3 p.m.

[3] Pilate's *gens*, the Pontii, was a Samnite *gens*. Had it been a Roman *gens* then I understand we should now be saying 'suffered under Quinctius Pilate', in the Creed.

On rune-height by the garbaged rill
       the scree-fall answers the cawed madrigals
and there are great birds flying about.
And (to sustain his kind)
           the mated corbie
with his neb
         forcipate, incarnadined—
prods at the dreaming *arbor*
          ornated *regis purpura* [1]
as his kind, should.
Each, after his kind, must somehow gain his kindly food:
ask of the mother thrush
          what brinded Tib has said.
What does the Gilyak tell
          to the gay-kerchiefed bear? [2]
They say he said he cared
          when sparrows fall—
shall he deny what's proper to the raven's bill:
          the hydromel
that moists the mortised *arbor*
         dry-stiped, *infelix*
trophy-fronded
         effluxed *et fulgida*? [1]
Who furthers the lammergyer? Who prevents the straight
crow-flight? Who goes before the doings of such kind of fowl?

---

[1] Cf. the Good Friday Liturgy, the hymn *Vexilla Regis*, '*Arbor decora et fulgida Ornata regis purpura.*' Tree beautiful and shining, made ornate with royal purple.

[2] Cf. the cult of the bear among hunting peoples of the north. Among the Tlingit Indians of Alaska the dead bear was decorated and addressed by the hunters: 'I am your friend, I am poor and come to you'. 'I am poor, that is why I am hunting you.' I have lost the reference to the coloured scarf with which in some cases the bear was adorned, but I think it was a practice of the Gilyaks of North-East Asia.

ONGYREDE·
hinε·þageonȝ
·hæleð:þæt·
wæs·god·✠
ælm·h·tig·
sȝrang·and
·stiðmod:
gestah·hε·on
·gealgan·he
annε:modig
on·manigrā
gesihðe:þa·he·wolde
·manncynn·lysan:

Had she been on Ariel mountain

                        would Selene

the Slumberer have refused

                        preferring, preferring
this Jugatinus of the noose, yoked for his nuptials on Skull
Ridge?[1]

On Ariel Hill, on Sion tumulus
on Uru Mound, in Salem cenacle
             in the white Beth-El
according to the *disciplina*
           of this peculiar people
in accord with the intentions
            of all peoples
and kindreds
et gentium, cenhedloedd,[2] *und Völker*

---

[1] See *England's Helicon* (1600) *Phyllida's Love Call*, verse 5.
    'Had my lovely one, my lovely one,
      Been in Ida plain—
    Cynthia Endymion had refused,
      Preferring, preferring
    My Corydon to play withal.'
And cf. where in *The City of God*, Bk. IV, 11, Augustine refers to Jugatinus
as one of gods of hill-sites, and in Bk. VI, 9, to Jugatinus the conjugal god.

[2] *cenhedloedd*, pronounce ken-hed-loith, th as in nether, plural of *cenedl*, a
kindred.

I use these terms: *gens, Volk, cenedl* as symbols of the three elements which
compose us. Together these three elements, broadly speaking, compose 'the
West': we are Germans, Latins, Celts and can apprehend only in a Latin,
Germanic and Celtic fashion. *What* we so apprehend, lay hold of—sciences,
principles, wisdoms, evangels from, e.g. Hellas at some remove, from Judaea
at a greater remove—that is another matter. *Gentes* other from us, of other
culture-groups, of other bloods and environments, have no doubt equally
significant and warm images. But even if I knew and could pronounce those alien
crucial-words, my list could not here extend beyond the three I have found
myself using, because they serve sufficiently, within the context, to cover what
is historically 'ours'. I am, of course, also thinking of Apocalypse V, 9, 'hast
redeemed us . . . out of every kindred and tongue and people and nation.'

that dance
> by garnished *Baum*

or anointed stone.
Here, in this place
> as in Sarras city

(where the maim was ended
> at the voyage-end) [1]

in his second Ephrata
here in the *upper* cave of bread [2]
between his creatures again his Body shows.
> At the low entry

stirs the sleeping dog?
in Bedlem-byre once his bed.
> (Long years beyond the twentieth year!) [3]

Here, in this high place
> into both hands [4]

he takes the stemmed dish
> as in many places

by this poured and that held up
wherever their directing glosses read:
> Here he takes the victim. [5]

---

[1] The allusion is to 'the Cyte of Sarras in the spyrytuel place' (Malory, Bk. XVII). It was at the city of Sarras that the Grail-quest was consummated, the Maimed King healed and from whence the lance and vessel were taken up to heaven.

[2] Cf. Homily 8, of the homilies on the Gospels by Pope Gregory the Great, where he speaks of the place-name Beth-Lehem, 'house of bread', with reference to our Lord as the bread of heaven. (Breviary, Christmas Day, Matins, 3rd Nocturn, Lesson VII.)

[3] Cf. *Odyssey* XVII 326-7, 'But the fate of black death overtook Argos immediately when he had seen Odysseus in the twentieth year.' Cf. note to page 192.

[4] See the rubric: *ambabus manibus accipit calicem* directing the celebrant how and when to take hold of the chalice about to be consecrated according to the Roman formulae.

[5] See *accipit hostiam*, the rubric which has already directed him—when he handled the bread to consecrate it.

At the threshold-stone
                    lifts the agéd head?
can toothless beast from stable come
                              discern the Child
in the Bread?

            But the fate of death?
Well, that fits The Gest:
            How else be coupled of this Wanderer
whose viatic bread shows forth a life?
            —in his well-built *megaron*.
If not by this Viander's own death's monument
by what bride-ale else lives his undying Margaron?
            —whose only threnody is Jugatine
and of the *thalamus:* reeds then! and minstrelsy.
            (Nor bid Anubis haste, but rather stay:
for he was whelped but to discern a lord's body).

He does what is done in many places
what he does other
            he does after the mode
of what has always been done.
What did he do other
            recumbent at the garnished supper?
What did he do yet other
            riding the Axile Tree?